Expressive Writing

Expressive Writing

Foundations of Practice

KATHLEEN ADAMS, EDITOR

ROWMAN & LITTLEFIELD EDUCATION
A Division of
ROWMAN & LITTLEFIELD PUBLISHERS, INC.
Lanham • *New York* • *Toronto* • *Plymouth, UK*

Published by Rowman & Littlefield Education
A division of Rowman & Littlefield Publishers, Inc.
A wholly owned subsidiary of The Rowman & Littlefield Publishing Group, Inc.
4501 Forbes Boulevard, Suite 200, Lanham, Maryland 20706
www.rowman.com

10 Thornbury Road, Plymouth PL6 7PP, United Kingdom

British Library Cataloguing in Publication Information Available

Library of Congress Cataloging-in-Publication Data
Adams, Kathleen, 1951-
   Expressive writing : foundations of practice / Kathleen Adams.
      pages cm. — (It's easy to W.R.I.T.E. expressive writing series ; 3)
   Includes bibliographical references.
   ISBN 978-1-4758-0311-2 (cloth : alk. paper) — ISBN 978-1-4758-0312-9 (pbk. : alk. paper) — ISBN 978-1-4758-0316-7 (electronic) 1. Diaries—Authorship. 2. Self-actualization (Psychology)—Problems, exercises, etc. I. Title.
   PN4390.A33 2013
   808.06'692—dc23
                                      2013017036

∞™ The paper used in this publication meets the minimum requirements of American National Standard for Information Sciences—Permanence of Paper for Printed Library Materials, ANSI/NISO Z39.48-1992.

Printed in the United States of America

Dedicated to

Robb Jackson, Ph.D., CJF, CAPF
1952-2013

You will go out in joy
and be led forth in peace;
the mountains and hills
will burst into song before you,
and all the trees of the field
will clap their hands.
Isaiah 55:12, NIV

Contents

Series Overview: About the *It's Easy to W.R.I.T.E.* Expressive Writing Series

Expressive writing originates from the writer's lived experience—past, present, or imagined future life. Written in the author's own voice, expressive writing creates bridges between thought and feeling, reason and intuition, idea and action. It is equally rooted in language arts and social science, and it takes multiple forms: journals, poetry, life story, personal essay, creative nonfiction, song lyrics, notes, and snippets of thought. Expressive writing is democratic and accessible. No special knowledge is needed, supplies are available and affordable, and research confirms that outcomes can be profound and even life-changing.

The *It's Easy to W.R.I.T.E.* Expressive Writing Series captures the voices of worldwide experts on the power of writing for personal development, academic improvement, and lasting behavioral change. Authors are both theorists and practitioners of the work they document, bringing real-life examples of practical techniques and stories of actual outcomes.

Individually or as a compendium, the volumes in the *It's Easy to W.R.I.T.E.* Expressive Writing Series represent thoughtful, innovative, demonstrated approaches to the myriad ways life-based writing can shape both critical thinking and emotional intelligence. Books in the series are designed to have versatile appeal for classroom teachers and administrators, health and behavioral health professionals, graduate programs that prepare educators and counselors, facilitators of expressive writing, and individuals who themselves write expressively. Workbooks offer well-crafted, self-paced writing programs for individual users, with facilitation guides and curricula for anyone who wishes to organize peer-writing circles to explore the material in community.

Each book or chapter author is held to exacting standards set by the series editor, Kathleen Adams, who, prior to her 1985 launch as a pioneer and global expert in the expressive writing field, was trained as a journalist and served as chief editor for a nonfiction publishing company.

It's Easy to W.R.I.T.E.

*W*hat do you want to write about? Name it. Write it down. (If you don't know, try one of these: *What's going on? How do I feel? What's on my mind? What do I want? What's the most important thing to do? What's the best/worst thing right now?*)

*R*econnect with your center. Close your eyes. Take three deep breaths. Focus. Relax your body and mind. Gather your thoughts, feelings, questions, ideas.

*I*nvestigate your thoughts and feelings. Start writing and keep writing. Follow the pen/keyboard. If you get stuck, close your eyes and recenter yourself. Reread what you've already written and continue. Try not to edit as you go; that can come later, if at all.

*T*ime yourself. Write for five to twenty minutes or whatever time you choose. Set the timer on your phone, stove, or computer. Plan another three to five minutes at the end for reflection.

*E*xit smart. Reread what you've written and reflect on it in a sentence or two: *As I read this, I notice . . .* or *I'm aware of . . .* or *I feel . . .* Note any action steps you might take or any prompts you might use for additional writes.

Foreword

It has been almost thirty years since the first expressive writing experiment was conducted. In that study, Sandra Beall and I discovered that putting emotional upheavals into words could actually improve people's physical health. Many of my colleagues in psychology and medicine were highly skeptical.

This may have been novel and controversial news in the scientific community, but people who had worked in the journaling world had discovered this truth on their own many years earlier. At the same time I was conducting those first expressive writing studies, Kathleen Adams and others were developing innovative journaling strategies that helped bring the art of writing to large audiences of people dealing with personal turmoil.

For the last thirty years, the worlds of experimental research and the practice of journaling have grown up together—sometimes in parallel and other times learning from each other. This marvelous book is written by some of the leading thinkers in the practice of expressive writing. Across the board, they have pioneered different approaches to writing that all seek similar outcomes: helping people to understand their plights and move beyond their pain. In all cases, the authors have found that translating emotional experiences into words can be freeing.

The science and the practice of expressive writing continue to complement one another. Science, which moves very slowly, is finding that many different approaches to expressive writing can improve physical and mental health for people dealing with a wide range of problems. Perhaps the most surprising laboratory results reveal that there is no single way that works best for everyone. One writing method may not work for you, but another may produce startling changes. For some, writing may not work at all.

If you are a practitioner or educator, this book will give you a broad picture of some of the methods that are currently available. If you are someone looking for guidance in writing, try out the various methods and see what works. And, if none of the methods fit exactly what you need, invent your own method and test it out.

This is the magic of expressive writing. It's a simple method that is relatively fast, quite inexpensive, and has the potential to change the way you see the world.

James W. Pennebaker, PhD
Regents Centennial Professor of Liberal Arts
Chair, Department of Psychology
University of Texas at Austin

Books by Dr. Pennebaker:
Opening Up: The Healing Power of Expressing Emotions
Writing to Heal: A Guided Journal for Recovering from Trauma and Emotional Upheaval
The Secret Life of Pronouns: What Our Words Say About Us

Preface

There is nothing so wise as a circle.

—*Rainer Maria Rilke*

Purpose

Although expressive writing has been an active part of both education and social science for several decades now, there has been, at best, a cordial acquaintance between the disciplines. Classroom teachers, faced with mandatory reporting requirements and uncertain of how to respond to and grade personal writing, may hesitate to invite disclosure of a student's actual lived experience. Counselors and therapists may suggest to clients that they write journals or poetry, but many do not have a teacher's skill in structuring a learning process.

One of my primary objectives for this inaugural volume in the expressive writing series was to create a larger conversation and to share ideas, experiences, and resources. I wanted this volume to offer perspectives on how expressive writing can be used for development of emotional intelligence, the capacity to assimilate and integrate learning, and the actualization of potential—shared goals of both education and psychotherapy.

Dr. Pennebaker's foreword articulates the thirty-year, intertwining history of expressive writing in social science research and applied practice. As he notes, the authors in this volume, although none of us had yet crossed paths, were laying the foundations of their own work in the field during the same years that he and his colleagues were conducting the earliest research experiments. The authors represent some of the most original thinking in the field—original not only in creative content but also in placement on the historical time line.

Who This Book Is For

There are several audiences for this book: classroom teachers; counselors and therapists; university programs that offer coursework in both education and psychotherapy; practitioners and facilitators; and writers who know or are discovering the power of expressive writing for healing, growth, and change.

If you are a classroom teacher, you will find inspiration and motivation to guide students to a more authentic place than tweets, texts, and Facebook posts can provide. It is ironic that the rapid pace of technology, which many feared would be inherently isolative, has instead created an explosion of personal writing, in which everyone now has equal opportunity to be an author with an audience. Expressive writing offers a respite from the noise. It invokes a quieter voice, an audience of one, an internally witnessed relationship with self built on person rather than *persona*. Emotional intelligence—and better writing—organically ensues.

If you are a counselor or therapist, you will learn standards-based theories and time-tested techniques of the pioneers in journal therapy, poetry therapy, and therapeutic writing. Journals have reached a tipping point of cultural acceptance. Clients, patients, and community groups are more attuned than ever before to the idea of writing as a way of releasing feelings and capturing life experience. This book is your essential guide to best practices, from those who have individually and collectively raised the bar.

If you are a university professor in education, social sciences, or guidance/counseling, you are preparing leaders of a generation for whom *persona* writing is a way of life. This text offers a comprehensive look at interdisciplinary ways in which expressive writing—deeper, perhaps more authentic—can be incorporated into a holistic philosophy of practice.

If you are a credentialed practitioner, community-based facilitator, writing coach, creative writing teacher, or other who brings this work to the world, you already know the radical nature of the work we do. You know the way that writing slices through the superficial and reveals what really matters. This book offers you eight master teachers, each bringing guidance and role modeling.

If you are yourself a writer, you have made an excellent choice! Settle in with a pot of tea or coffee and a full inkwell, and prepare to be absorbed.

What You Will Learn

The volume opens with a true pioneer—the groundbreaking Dr. James W. Pennebaker—in his foreword. His influence continues in chapter 1, "Expression and Reflection," which opens with my review of his research model, after which I place the research into a counseling context with specific suggestions for harvesting insight and synthesizing cognitive change.

Dr. Robb Jackson is the sort of college professor that even the most skeptical student respects and trusts. The walls of his office are papered with scrawled notes, art, and posters. Each is an offering from a student who feels smart, soothed, and creatively supported in Robb's presence. They call him "the Shoobeedoo Man" after his riffs on how the best writing comes from the *shoobeedoo,* the never-ending inner flow, as rhythmic and true as a drumbeat. Chapter 2, "Finding Your *Shoobeedoo,*" takes the reader into a delicious slipstream of story, philosophy, and voice.

One of my most enduring contributions to the field of expressive and therapeutic writing is a developmental continuum theory called "the Journal Ladder." Chapter 3 discusses the concepts of structure, pacing, and containment as vital tools in the expressive writing process. It offers new detail on the nuances of the ladder and its applications for writers at all levels of skill and willingness.

Kate Thompson, an established expert on therapeutic journal writing in both the United Kingdom and the United States, puts the journal ladder into action in chapter 4, "Journal Writing in the Counseling Relationship." Through mini case studies and profound journal entries, Kate reveals the powerful workings of expressive writing during or after a counseling session and shares keen insight on how teachers, clinicians, and facilitators can use journals for self-supervision.

Since 2003, Joy Roulier Sawyer and I have taught poetry therapy together, both in professional training and also in a liberal studies master's program at the University of Denver. In chapter 5, "Liberating Beauty," Joy introduces the theory of developmental poetry therapy as crafted by pioneers Arleen Hynes and Mary Hynes-Berry in their classic text, *Biblio/Poetry Therapy*. She concludes with an applied-practice view of the model as used in an actual classroom setting.

Throughout her career as a community college counselor, Linda Barnes has taught expressive writing as a means to writing skill development. In chapter 6, "Engaging the Reluctant Writer," she shares techniques and word games that turn underdeveloped writers into active, engaged authors of their own experience.

Dr. Perie Longo, poet laureate *emerita* of Santa Barbara, has taught poetry to children through the California Poets in the Schools program since the mid-1980s. Chapter 7, "Poetry and Emotional Intelligence," demonstrates the power of poetic expression to help children wrap language around intense emotions and complex thoughts. Try not to read ahead to the actual poems of primary school children, written on themes such as discovery, stress, identity, and collective trauma.

In 1992, Richard Gold founded the Pongo Teen Writing Project. The project is dedicated to offering mentored poetry writing to adolescents who have experienced childhood traumas such as abuse and neglect, thus giving teen authors opportunities to safely write about experiences that have been hard to talk about. In chapter 8, "Expressive Writing with Teens at Risk," Richard describes the Pongo model that has served more than six thousand youth in juvenile detention centers, homeless shelters, and psychiatric hospitals.

If all expressive writing begins with personal story, then perhaps all personal stories begin with "Writing Your Family Story" (chapter 9). Family therapist and memoirist Dr. Linda Joy Myers concludes the volume with rich experience and juicy story starters for family members of all ages and stages.

"There Is Nothing So Wise as a Circle": Expressive Writing and Community

In 1985 I called my first journal circle. Six of my friends sat on my living room floor and wrote their hearts out and shared their stories. I was a first-semester graduate student in a counseling program, and I knew in that inaugural writing group that the intersection of personal healing and journal writing was my life's work.

I have always done my work in community. I am a natural weaver of lives; I am a gatherer of overlapping, intersecting circles of those who speak on the page, who read their stories in voices that quaver or whisper or soar, in the presence of witnesses who receive without judgment and respond with compassion.

This is what I have learned in writing circles across the decades and around the world: Expressive writing changes us. It brings peace to our hearts. It restores balance. Writing connects us to the parts of ourselves that have been lost, abandoned, neglected, forgotten, or ignored. We learn that there are wise, friendly, and sensible selves within us that want us to succeed. They are willing to share their wisdom with us. Writing is the bridge.

Community also changes us. We learn that we are not alone. We see ourselves reflected in another's shining eyes. We hold for each other what we cannot reliably hang onto for ourselves. We learn that we are enough, we are sufficient, we have something to say and a voice with which to say it.

Dr. Pennebaker states in his foreword that expressive writing "has the potential to change the way you see the world." I believe that writing communities—in classrooms, conference rooms, family rooms, therapists' offices, places of worship, community centers, coffee shops—have the power to deepen and accelerate the process of change. And what might arise from a collectively shifted worldview?

My vision for this book is that it will substantially advance the dialogue about the role of expressive writing for healing, growth, and change at every level: individual, family, community, country, culture, world.

And so begins the conversation. I hope you will add your voice.

Kathleen Adams, MA, LPC
Series Editor, *It's Easy to W.R.I.T.E.* Expressive Writing Series
Join the dialogue:
www.itseasytowrite.com
kathleen@itseasytowrite.com

1

Expression and Reflection: Toward a New Paradigm in Expressive Writing

KATHLEEN ADAMS

Amber is a twenty-six-year-old woman with a bad-tempered boyfriend; she's dated him for just over a year. She comes to me for counseling because her doctor has prescribed antianxiety medication and told her to get some help. In our first session, I explain that expressive writing is a primary tool in my practice. I ask her to write for five minutes, describing the relationship in her own words. What's working? What's not working?

For the first minute, her writing is halting and jerky. Then she raises her head, stares past me out the window, takes a deep breath, and dives in. Her pen doesn't stop until I call time.

I ask her to read to me. She pours out a river of words that express her conflict about the relationship. She knows it might not be healthy. She loves him. If only he would be kinder and more patient, she is sure they could make it work. The vibrations of her words in her own voice linger in the air. When the reverberations have faded, I ask her to write another sentence or two of reflection: What does she notice about the writing and the reading? She turns to the page again and writes slowly. She reads her reflection: "I notice that I'm the only one who becomes kinder and more patient. He never does. I'm scared he never will."

Our work has begun.

What it is about writing our stories—our own lived experience, our own words, our own voice, our own truth—that makes us feel stronger and more in touch with ourselves?

According to the preeminent researcher in the expressive writing field, James W. Pennebaker, and Janel Seagal (1999), "[Keeping] a journal may facilitate the process of forming a narrative about . . . experiences, as well as reinforce progress, and support the change of maladaptive behaviors" (1251).

I have specialized in this field since 1985, when, as a first-year counseling graduate student, I taught my first journal workshop in my living room to six friends. I knew immediately that the intersection of writing and therapy was my life's work. Since then, my work has been devoted to offering the healing art and science of expressive writing to all who desire self-directed change.

I define expressive writing[1] as writing that reflects honest thoughts and feelings about authentic lived experience, with a side of insight. In this definition, trauma and stress are excellent topics, and so are hopes and dreams, confusions, confessions, secrets, successes, troubles, ideas, desires, and the "everyday normals" that comprise a life. The outcomes arising from this definition bring writers into real-time awareness of thoughts, feelings, and behaviors. Through a follow-on reflection write,[2] this awareness can be harvested as insight, an important ingredient in the change process. Thus, the write, and its reflection, become powerful catalysts for growth and change.

Since 2006, I have traveled to more than 120 U.S. cities in forty-three states, bringing a one-day workshop on the theory and practice of journal therapy to more than 6,500 therapists, counselors, and facilitators. Each time I teach, I ask the audience to complete the sentence stem, *When my clients or students write journals* . . . These three responses frequently occur:

1. Clients/students develop insight and awareness.
2. They are better able to express and regulate emotions.
3. Clients/students move through treatment more quickly. More work gets done in less time when they continue the work between sessions.

And all of these benefits are *before* I teach them about reflection writes.

Expressive writing and follow-on reflection offer accessible pathways to different and better thoughts, feelings, emotions, and experiences. As a client once told me, "Writing a journal is like having a box of magic wands."

The Research: The Early Years

Social science research on expressive writing[3] dates from the mid-1980s. It was then that the first landmark study was published correlating emotional release, or expressive, writing with improvement in overall health functioning (Pennebaker and Beall 1986). Over the next several years, expressive writing studies carved out a method that would hold up across three decades and hundreds of applications. Three or four segments of writing, each taking fifteen to twenty minutes, were typically spaced one day apart.[4] All but a few studies included random assignments of participants to one or more experimental expressive writing group(s) or to a control group that wrote about deliberately neutral, mundane, or superficial topics. In most of the early studies, experimental writers were instructed to "write deeply" about a topic that was both emotionally difficult and difficult to share. Early on, the data established that writing about both content and affect (as opposed to only about the facts of the story, or only about the emotions experienced) offered the best outcomes, so experimental writers were typically instructed to include both facts and feelings (Pennebaker 1989).

The health benefits from the initial studies were promising indeed: increased immune system function, fewer visits to health care providers for illnesses, lowered blood pressure, improved heart rate, increased antibodies for Epstein-Barr and hepatitis B patients, and other physiological improvements (Smyth 1998). Because of the cathartic nature of writing deeply about difficult, often traumatic, material, the earliest theories conceptualized the expressive writing process as a release valve that depressurized inhibition through the silent "confession" of deeply troubling material. Pennebaker and Beall wrote:

> [Statistical analyses alone do not] convey the powerful and personal nature of the majority of trauma condition essays. One woman wrote about teaching her brother to sail; on his first solo outing, he drowned. The father of a male subject separated from his mother when the subject was about 9 years old. Prior to leaving home, the father told the subject that the divorce was the subject's fault. . . . When she was 10 years old, one female subject had been asked to clean her room because her grandmother was to be visiting that night. The girl did not do so. That

night, the grandmother tripped on one of the girl's toys, broke her hip, and died of complications during surgery a week later. . . . Another [subject], who had written about relatively trivial topics during the first sessions, admitted during the last [writing session] that she was gay. A male subject reported that he had considered suicide because he thought that he had disappointed his parents. (1986, 277)

The 1986 study also included a form of reflection. At a four-month follow-up, subjects were asked to respond to the question, "Looking back on the experiment, do you feel as if it has had any long-lasting effects? Please answer this in your own words." The responses to the open-ended question were "uniformly positive" and included these responses:

It helped me think about what I felt during those times. I never realized how it affected me before.

It helped to write things out when I was tense, so now when I'm worried I sit and write it out. . . . Later, I feel better.

I had to think and resolve past experiences. . . . One result of the experiment is peace of mind, and a method to relieve emotional experiences. To have to write emotions and feelings helped me understand how I felt and why.

Although I have not talked with anyone about what I wrote, I was finally able to deal with it, work through the pain instead of trying to block it out. Now it doesn't hurt to think about it. (Pennebaker and Beall 1986, 279)

A study designed to assess whether expressive writing helped incoming college freshmen better cope with the first semester of college (Pennebaker et al. 1990) had experimental participants write essays for three consecutive days about

. . . your very deepest thoughts and feelings about coming to college. . . . In your writing, you might want to write about your emotions and thoughts about leaving your friends or your parents, about issues of adjusting to the various aspects of college such as roommates, classes, or thoughts about your future, or even about your feelings of who you are or what you want to become. The important thing is that you really let go and dig down to your very deepest emotions and thoughts and explore them in your writing (531).

The most common themes of the essays included existential issues such as feelings of isolation and loneliness (54 percent of subjects discussed this in at least one essay); loss of family (51 percent); loss of friends back home (45 percent); general worries about the future (42 percent); general academic concerns (41 percent); issues surrounding identity such as "who am I?" (39 percent) (532).

As with the 1986 study, subjects were asked at follow-up to respond to an open-ended question about "how [the experiment] may have influenced you in the long run." Only 10 percent discussed the value of writing in venting terms (e.g., "I purged some of my feelings" or "I had a chance to get my feelings out in the open"). The vast majority (76 percent) described the long-term effects by referring to their achieving insight (e.g., "It made me think things out and really realize what my problem is"; "It helped me look at myself from the outside"; and "It was a chance to sort out my thoughts") (534).

Thus, at least some of the earliest experiments included an opportunity for the participants to reflect on the process of writing and how it may have served them.

Through the first decade of the writing experiments, it was becoming clear that catharsis seemed to seek the container of story, and that the arc of the three or four essays seemed to organize thoughts and feelings into a coherent, consistent narrative. Pennebaker and Seagal (1999) wrote:

[The process of constructing story] allows one to organize and remember events in a coherent fashion while integrating thoughts and feelings. In essence, this gives individuals a sense of predictability and control over their lives. Once an experience has structure and meaning, it would follow that the emotional effects of that experience are more manageable. Constructing stories facilitates a sense of resolution, which results in less rumination and eventually allows disturbing experiences to subside gradually from conscious thought. Painful events that are not structured into a narrative format may contribute to the continued experience of negative thoughts and feelings. (1243)

One of the earliest systematic approaches to understanding the potential cognitive effects of writing was to have independent raters read the essays and assess them for qualities such as self-reflection, emotional openness, and thoughtful interpretation. "Not being content with clinical evaluations," the authors wrote, "we decided to subject the essays to computer-text analysis to learn if language use could predict improvements in health among people who had written about emotional topics" (1248).

The Next Stage: Linguistic Analysis

In order to study the individual components of narrative, Pennebaker and several colleagues "spent three years developing a computer program called Linguistic Inquiry and Word Count (LIWC) that analyzed essays in text format (Pennebaker and Francis, 1996)" (Pennebaker and Seagal 1999, 1248). LIWC's vast database included words that signaled cognition, positive emotion, negative emotion, belief, causality, and insight. For each essay, LIWC could "quickly compute the percentage of total words that these and other linguistic categories presented" (1248).

The early findings looked at the emotion words and the cognitive words in subjects' essays. With LIWC's help, they found that people who used a moderate number of negative emotion words in their writing went to the doctor less often than those who used a lot, or very few, negative words. In the cognitive word categories, the investigators found:

> The LIWC analyses showed strong and consistent effects for changes in insight and causal words over the course of writing. Specifically, people whose health improved, who got higher grades, and who found jobs after writing went from using relatively few causal and insight words to using a high rate of them by the last day of writing. In reading the essays of people who showed this pattern of language use, it became apparent that they were constructing a story over time. Building a narrative, then, seemed to be critical in reaching understanding. (1249)

When understanding is reached, and thoughts are organized into a coherent, cohesive narrative, insight and meaning are accessible. The authors continue:

> The beauty of a narrative is that it allows us to tie all of the changes in our life into a broad comprehensive story. That is, in the same story we can talk both about the cause of the event and its many implications. Much as in any story

there can be overarching themes, plots, and subplots—many of them arranged logically and/or hierarchically. Through this process, the many facets of the presumed single event are organized into a more coherent whole. (1250)

Poon and Danoff-Burg (2011) offered mindfulness ("paying complete attention to the experiences occurring presently, in a nonjudgmental way or an accepting stance") as a moderator that might deepen the writer's capacity to create insight and meaning. Study participants completed several inventories, including the Freiberg Mindfulness Inventory that measures mindfulness as a personality trait, before following instructions to write three times over several days, for twenty minutes each time, about a stressful experience.

Mindfulness influenced the extent of benefits produced by expressive writing. . . . [A] higher mindfulness score predicted greater change over time in decreased physical symptoms, decreased psychological symptoms, and decreased negative affect, but an increase in sleep quality and positive affect. These findings suggest that people who are more mindful benefit more from disclosing their emotions and thoughts regarding stressful experiences than do those who are less mindful. (890)

The Third Wave: Challenging Assumptions

In nearly every study, the writing task is organized around an experience or event from the writer's life that is deemed traumatic, stressful, troubling, secretive, or/and difficult. Greenberg et al. (1996) brought fresh perspectives to the theoretical dialogue by having participants write about fictional traumas, "upsetting events that [they] had not personally experienced and that were encountered for the first time during the experiment" (589). The positive outcomes were indeed similar to those of the group that wrote about actual trauma, and the authors suggested that writing about fictional trauma may enhance the capacity to regulate feelings and/or construct a more resilient "possible self" (599).

King and Miner (2000) also challenged the assumption that writing about one's own traumatic events or negative emotions was a necessary component. Their study showed that those who wrote about the perceived benefits of a trauma ("the positive aspects and how the experience has benefited you as a person—how has the experience made you better able to meet the challenges of the future?" [223]) had the same physical benefits as those who wrote about loss or trauma.

> Results of the computerized analyses (LIWC) and ratings made by independent judges showed that those in the trauma-only and perceived-benefits-only conditions wrote in dissimilar ways. Those in the perceived-benefits-only group used significantly more positive emotion words and more words indicating cognitive insight than did those in the trauma-only group. In addition, trauma-only essays were rated as more traumatic, less positive, more negative, and less resolved than were perceived-benefits-only essays. Thus, it does not appear that the similar health results are due to similarities in writing. Essays written in the perceived-benefits condition were, quite simply, more positive than were those written in the trauma conditions. . . . [W]riting about the positive aspects of the event [may] allow participants to gain a sense of efficacy in terms of their cognitive capacities to find meaning in the event. (227)

King continued her exploration of writing about self-regulatory topics with a 2001 study comparing the health benefits of writing about trauma with writing about life goals. Her findings:

> Results indicate that writing about life goals is another way to enjoy the health benefits of writing without the emotional costs. Indeed, writing about one's life goals was associated with feeling less upset, more happy, and getting sick less often. . . . [T]he physical benefits . . . were equal to or better than writing about trauma, whereas writing about a traumatic life event also entailed feeling upset and experiencing lowered mood. . . . It may be possible to enjoy the benefits of writing without necessarily writing about trauma at all. (805)

Burton and King (2004) asked experimental subjects to write about non-emotional topics or intensely positive experiences (IPEs) for twenty minutes each over three consecutive days. IPE writers showed increased positive mood, LIWC analyses revealed that their language reflected positive and insightful aspects, and everyone in the IPE portion of the study remained healthy. However,

> *none* of the mediational analyses were successful in identifying the underlying mechanisms of this effect. Thus, this study, like others using the disclosive writing paradigm, indicates that writing "works"—i.e., it is associated with superior health—but does not provide a strong indication for why this is so (King 2002).[5] This study broadens our appreciation for the "healing power of writing." Writing about life experience may have more general implications than have previously been explored. Furthermore, our results suggest that the discussion about the potential mechanisms of the writing effects should be broadened to include a variety of processes that are not exclusive to confronting life events. (159–61)

The Research as Applied to Clinical Practice

Greenberg et al., King, Miner, and Burton extended the convention of writing primarily about traumatic, stressful, or negative experiences. However, none of the studies to date have attempted to extend beyond the convention of three or four writes. It doesn't surprise me that such a brief intervention is effective. But it does surprise me that a longer number of writes has not been suggested as a moderator for effects. If three days are good, how great might three weeks be? Or three months? Three seasons? Three years? What about writing as preventative health care? Writing as a daily or weekly debrief with the self? Writing as a marker of consciousness and change? Writing as a reliable, silent friend at 3:00 a.m.? What about expressive writing as a lifestyle?

Here's a typical Tuesday in my private practice. My first client is "Johnny," who doesn't really like to write but will if I "make" him. (That's his way of asking for the witnessing, guidance, structure, and support that he is not reliably able to provide for himself.) Since he seldom fails to tell himself something useful when he writes, I "make" him write in nearly every session. Usually I wait until there's a juicy moment in the therapeutic conversation, when I can see he is teetering on the edge of connecting the dots. "Clean page!" I bark.

"Give me five minutes on . . ." whatever it is that he is ready to see, know, recognize, acknowledge, glimpse, or integrate.

He reads what he's written to me, and we carry on, deepening his connection with this newfound whatever-it-is, and for homework I ask him to write, on three different days, a list of three different gratitudes.

Next is "Amber," still with her boyfriend three months later. Today she can barely stay in her skin with guilt and anxiety. We begin with a quick check-in write, two sentence stems, *Today I want to work on . . .* and *Since our last session . . .* She writes that she revealed to herself in her journal this week that it is time to break up with her boyfriend. We sit in silence while she weeps. Then we get to work. Amber wants to work on how to tell her boyfriend. She writes out several openings. We role-play each one. She revises after each round until she gets it right. She won't forget what she wanted to say; it's written down.

After lunch it's "Mindy," back into therapy after a relapse and maintaining a shaky sobriety. She is working on the first three steps of Alcoholics Anonymous in her journal, writing herself letters from God (who, in Mindy's letters, is female) and making long lists of her fears about powerlessness and unmanageability and restoration to sanity. She likes writing lists, she tells me, because they are just one or two words and that's not as overwhelming as a whole thought. She also likes the straight spine of the numbers marching down the page; that structure soothes her. We spend the session on family-of-origin issues that have surfaced since we last met. Fortunately, she brought her journal, so she can accurately reconstruct time and process.

Next I meet with "Tony," a bipolar tattoo artist who rides high on his mania and then crashes into the pit. He has a hard time working when he's manic, so he's learned to cluster (mind map) his racing thoughts. Being able to trap them in bubbles on the page and connect them with lines to other bubbles helps him think straight and compartmentalize his flighty ideas. When he's "down" (depressed), it's hard to talk, and he draws icons, cartoons, bumper stickers, tattoo designs. Today he's down. I hand him the basket of colored pencils, and he swiftly sketches out the week just past. Before the hour is over, he has added a sentence or two to each of his scenes, and he's sketched out the plan we've made for the week upcoming.

My last client is "Nicole." This is our third session. She comes to me through the county victim's assistance program; she was raped. In the second session we focused on building internal resources—a safe place, an inner ally—and today we will move into the story. I have chosen for her the classic

Pennebaker four-part write (2004), adapted for this clinical task. Like the investigators who do research studies, I begin by describing the process we'll go through. Then I guide her through a closed-eye entrance meditation (Progoff 1992) to activate her safe place. We break the story into tiny bits, five to seven minutes each, writing without reflection but with a few minutes of verbal check-in and processing after each round. When the last write is completed, she reads all four pieces out loud. She has told me her story. We close with a reflection, in which she writes that she is shaken but relieved.

Each client writes (sometimes Tony draws) reflections at the end of their writing, or at the end of the session. My verbal instructions that prompt the reflection write usually include the direction to "reread what you've written, and pay attention to what you notice, or what surprises you, stands out for you, suddenly makes sense, or is something you didn't know you knew." The reflection offers opportunities for synthesis, integration, awareness, insight, and self-determination. In my experience, it amplifies all other benefits to the writing process.

Although I have worked with many clients with devastating trauma stories, I have worked with just as many who come in with "everyday normal" stresses—the ongoing griefs and grinds that we shoulder as part of current reality. Shattered trust, bleak moods, addictions and dependencies, painful circumstances, communication impasses, family breakdowns, health challenges, uncertain futures, untenable workplaces, wayward children, financial despair, chronic stress—these are the sorts of problems my clients lean into, with varying success, every day. They want movement, and they want it fast.

That's where expressive writing can really shine. Three conventions that have become standards for me as I offer writing to my clients, students, and workshop participants are:

Choices in technique. The availability of a variety of writing techniques, each with particular properties and benefits, allows the writer or facilitator to choose a technique that supports a desired outcome. Chapter 3, "The Journal Ladder," details the choices and the choice-making process.

Recognizing changes in feelings. I constantly teach my clients a basic therapeutic truth: Feelings change with time and process. Moods are more intractable, but feelings are fluid. Writing three words that describe the feeling state at the beginning of a journal entry, and three feeling words again at the end of the reflection, offer immediate feedback about how a process (writing and reflection) can allow a change in feelings over not very much time (five to twenty minutes, usually). Although manipulation of emotional state is not the point of this process, the most common outcome for my clients is that they feel different, and better, after they write. This contrasts with much of the literature that suggests it is common for experimental subjects to feel worse after writing (Pennebaker 2000).

Reflection. It would be difficult to overstate the value of written reflection. The earliest studies noted the emergence of insight when subjects were asked open-ended questions about process. Poon and Danoff-Burg raise mindfulness as a moderator for the expressive writing paradigm. As LIWC has become a standard feature of research design, the essays from studies have been analyzed for insight and causal cognition, as well as positive and negative emotion words. This is an enormous contribution. However, my experience is that the insight, awareness, and cognitive shift from the write itself are amplified, multiplied, synthesized, and codified in the reflection write.

To demonstrate these points, I designed a small study[6] that addressed the questions:

1. Do feelings shift between the start of a write and the end of the reflection? If so, is there a pattern or trend to the shift?
2. What is the effect of the classic four-part expressive writing model on "everyday normal" problems?
3. Do reflection writes, independent of the writes themselves, demonstrate insight, synthesis, changes in beliefs/attitudes/behaviors, improved self-concept, better self-regulation, or/and action orientation?

The "Everyday Normal" Writing Project

Overview

Twenty-three adult volunteers were asked to write in the classic four-part expressive writing research pattern over the course of one week. Each participant was asked to choose one "everyday normal" stress, issue, or activity, defined as "something that is real and present in your everyday life, but that is incorporated into your daily flow without causing undue hardship or difficulty." Participants were specifically instructed: "Do not choose a topic that activates or intensifies emotional pain, anger or shame. 'Everyday' feelings, such as annoyance, regret, conflict, frustration, confusion, or guilt are 'normal' for this project." Pleasurable topics were also encouraged. It was suggested that participants choose one of three types of experience:

- a *chronic* (long-term) issue or challenge, such as a health, family, financial, or workplace matter (chosen by twelve participants)
- an *acute* (finite) incident that is absorbing time, energy, and focus, such as a project, upcoming event, decision, or mild crisis (chosen by seven participants)
- a *positive* pleasure, hobby, or practice, such as gardening, photography, or meditation (chosen by four participants)

At the beginning of each writing session, participants were instructed to write any three *feeling words* that described their emotional mood or state as they contemplated their chosen topic. Additionally, as the participants finished each write, they were asked to reread their writing and add a *reflection* that focused on the process of writing and observed details such as physical and emotional responses to the write, surprises, "aha" moments, and notations about areas for further exploration. After the reflection was completed, participants again chose any three feeling words that described their emotional mood or state as of the end of the entire writing process (content plus reflection). Participants were asked to schedule uninterrupted thirty-minute segments for each writing session, divided into fifteen to eighteen minutes for the initial write, three to four minutes to reread, and five to ten minutes for the reflection write. All four writes/reflections were to be completed in one week.

Procedure

Participants were given written instructions by email about how to approach each of the four writes. These instructions were adapted from a journal therapy clinical protocol (Adams 2006; see table 1.1), in turn adapted from standard expressive writing protocols (Pennebaker 2004). The Pennebaker-style

Table 1.1. Adams Interpretation of Pennebaker Writing Instructions (Adams 2006)

Write 1	Tell the story of what happened. Write without regard for grammar, punctuation, spelling, etc. Include both facts and feelings.
Write 2	Tell more of the story. Add in layers through details and parts of the story often omitted. Continue writing both content (facts) and affect (feelings).
Write 3	How has this story impacted your life? What has it meant to you? How does it continue to shape you? Are there experiences, activities, or behaviors you move toward or away from as a result of this experience?
Write 4	Where do you go from here? How do you feel about this event and its impact, now that you've spent time exploring it? Is there action to take? Synthesize.

instructions typically invite exploration of "deepest thoughts and feelings" on day one with instructions to continue exploration of deepest thoughts and feelings for successive days. The adapted journal therapy instructions given to participants are summarized as:

Write #1. Write for fifteen to eighteen minutes about the topic you have chosen. Write without regard for punctuation, spelling, grammar, etc. You may write by hand or on a computer. Write both facts and feelings. Just tell the story that the chosen topic represents in your life. When fifteen to eighteen minutes have passed and you are at a stopping place, reread what you have written, and write your reflection piece for five to ten minutes.

Write #2. Write for fifteen to eighteen minutes about the chosen topic, but this time add in "layers"—details you missed in Write 1, contexts, outside or internal influences. Again, write both content (the story) and affect (how you feel about the story). When you have completed this, reread what you have written, and write your reflection piece for five to ten minutes.

Write #3. Write for fifteen to eighteen minutes about the chosen topic, this time exploring meaning. What does it mean to have this topic as a part of your "everyday normal"? How has this topic impacted you? What do you move toward or away from as a result of this topic?

Write #4. In this final write of fifteen to eighteen minutes, synthesize your thinking and contemplate a move into action. Having explored this topic for three writes and reflections, what do you see freshly or differently? What insights have you gained? Are there action steps you might take? What might you keep, and what might you cut away? What, if anything, has changed or shifted? When you have completed this, reflect one last time, both on this synthesis and on the process as a whole.

Instructions for the reflection write were:

Reflection write. Each time you complete a write, you will continue by immediately rereading what you have written and writing a reflection. The reflection focuses on the process of writing, as filtered through cognitive, physical, or/and emotional channels. Describe your process as accurately and in as much detail as you can. Poetic truth, metaphor, nonphysical realities, and sensations are valid, as are more rational descriptions and reports. . . . [Topics addressed may include] What do you notice immediately, upon rereading? Were there any surprises? Any "aha" moments or insights? Did you experience shifts cognitively, emotionally, or physically? What happened as you wrote?

Participants were instructed to return only the reflection write, along with the before-and-after sets of feeling words, for each write. The actual writes themselves were not requested and were disregarded if submitted.

Measurement of Affective Shift from Writing

The twenty-three subjects each wrote eight sets of three feeling words (twenty-four words for each participant, or 552 words collectively) to describe their affective states before the writes and after the reflections. Feelings were sorted into five categories. Each category was assigned a value (see table 1.2).

Thus, values for a three-word set could range from three (all "disempowering" feeling words) to fifteen (all "empowering" feeling words). Statistical analysis measured trends and changes from prewrite to postwrite across the writes, and for each of the four writes.

Table 1.2. Distribution of Feeling Words

Category of feeling word	Sample feeling words in category	Words (N = 552)	Percent	Value per word
Disempowering	Angry, anxious, fearful, hopeless, pain, shame	75	13.59	1
Somewhat disempowering	Annoyed, confused, disappointed, listless, nervous, worried	114	20.65	2
Neutral	Ambivalent, cautious, interested, searching, surprised, wondering	71	12.86	3
Somewhat empowering	Amazed, curious, eager, reassured, satisfied, willing	111	20.11	4
Empowering	Blessed, committed, empowered, joyful, motivated, strong	181	32.79	5

There was a significant upward trend of prewrite scores across the writes. The prewrite scores at Write 4 (10.78 out of 15) compared to Write 1 (7.70 out of 15) demonstrate that participants began their last writing process in a slightly better than neutral emotional place, compared to the mildly disempowering place in which they began the first write.

The postwrite trend test also indicated a significant upward trend across the writes; the postwrite scores at Write 4 were significantly higher than any other postwrite score.

The change from prewrite 1 (7.7) to postwrite 4 (13.1) indicates an emotional shift from "somewhat disempowering" to "somewhat empowering" over the course of the one-week writing intervention, a shift that showed no change at a two-week follow-up.

Documenting Change through Reflection

The *process* of this affective change is documented in the reflection writes. This is the introspective voice, the observing ego, the silent witness to internal experience. The reflection write specifically invites insight, and it does so through the writer's own observation of process. In the excerpted reflections following, note the articulations of awareness, recognition, insight, and the potential for change.

Participant Four is a retired woman with a wide social network. She eats out often with her friends. Her "everyday normal" problem was the frequent opportunity and subtle peer pressure to eat rich, high-calorie foods instead of following healthier eating patterns.

Write 1. Starting words: Anxious, eager, ready. *Reflection:* Writing about this made me more aware of my "excuses" habit and made me more determined to do the things that are in my best self-interest. *Ending words:* Relaxed, aware, determined.

Write 2. Starting words: Satisfied, aware, stimulated. *Reflection:* I had quite a philosophical discussion with myself about self-interest and what it means to me. . . . I might compromise what is in my healthy self-interest in order to get along with other people. . . . This writing is making me look at the larger picture to see what I might be able to do to meet my own needs without offending or alienating others. *Ending words:* Curious, motivated, relieved.

Write 3. Starting words: Uncertain, frustrated, ambivalent. *Reflection:* Today I noticed I wrote more about my feelings toward the choices I make—from my head or my heart? I noticed a shift in my feelings from being a victim or used by others to becoming my own person. *Ending words:* Energized, calm, confident.

Write 4. Starting words: Quiet, confident, satisfied. *Reflection:* I now feel more empowered to do what I've always known is the right thing to do for myself. The choices are mine (as I've always known they were) but now I have a plan in place that is in my own best interests and will not offend others. *Ending words:* Happy, motivated, calm.

Across four reflections, Participant Four challenged her "excuses habit" and made note of her determination to change her behavior. She reached deep to explore the underlying meaning of her choices. She observed herself shift away from a feeling of victimization and toward a feeling of self-reliance. She prepared herself for new behavior by creating a plan to make different choices in a socially graceful way. At the two-week follow-up, Participant Four reflected:

> It felt good to look back on the outcome of writing about the impact of my diet choices on my well-being. I feel much better about myself—and my friends— than I did before writing. The experience of writing gave me some much-needed backbone that enabled me to speak up and take better care of myself. . . . [The experience] reinforced in my mind what I had decided that I wanted and needed to do for myself. I feel stronger and more in charge of what matters most to me—my health and well-being.

Participant Fifteen has "struggled for years" with dysthymia (a form of chronic depression in which mood is often described as low, dark, or sad) and has "journaled about it countless times."

Write 1. Starting words: Eager, anxious, hopeful. *Reflection:* A new insight came when I wrote about "hiding" it. [I didn't realize the extent to which I have been] struggling with it alone. Keeping up the front. Not wanting anyone to see it. Pretending it's not there. All of my attempts to keep it a secret—that was new awareness. I've never made this connection before. *Ending words:* Frustrated, confused, hopeful.

Write 2. Starting words: Worried, frustrated, tired. *Reflection:* An "aha" moment for me was realizing that I seemed to have chosen "serious and important" people to model my life after, people who may have actually been depressed. I'm beginning to think that they were also my role models for a mood disorder. A radically new and strangely empowering concept. *Ending words:* Foolish, hopeful, cautious.

Write 3. Starting words: Excited, frightened, hopeful. *Reflection:* No new insights, exactly, but understanding things at a deeper level. And a readiness now to be able to put these things into action and actually give up my old tired narrative and write a new one consistent with what I believe now rather than continuing to play out the old narrative based on things I no longer believe and no longer serve me well. *Ending words:* Excited, optimistic, joyful.

Write 4. Starting words: Enlightened, clear-headed, strong. *Reflection:* What I notice most is . . . having an action plan that is actually exciting and without the sense of dread. I feel strongly that I am on to something. I seem to have gotten to some truths about myself and things I have been struggling with for a long, long time. I'm not sure I understand how it all happened, but somehow it just did. New awareness seems to have bubbled up . . . Putting things into action and making change is harder than thinking/writing about it. But I will work hard to remember what I've learned. To remember that I have a choice. *Ending words:* Excited, optimistic, empowered.

Participant Fifteen's immediate insight about "hiding" her depression from others led to a thoughtful examination of the way that, as a child, she gravitated to role models who may have themselves been depressed, and how she may have imprinted some of their emotional patterns. This awareness progressed into acknowledgment of the readiness to retire an old narrative and write a new narrative, more congruent with her adult perception. She ends with acknowledgment that insight alone does not lead to change and vows to "work hard to remember" that she has choices. At the two-week follow-up, Participant Fifteen wrote:

> My biggest fear when I completed the four writes was that some of my new insights and resultant changes in moods would not last and would never make it to becoming changes in behavior. But so far, it's been really different. I've caught myself numerous times during the past two weeks remembering my new insights and doing something different. And I didn't replace negative crap with positive self-talk. I didn't replace it with a cheery affirmation. It was stronger and more powerful than that. It was more a nonverbal sense or *awareness* that everything really is okay and that I *can* do this and do it *without any angst.* And then I'd simply go about doing the business of whatever it was I had to do. This wasn't part of my action plan. It just occurred naturally.

> So how does this work? How did this act of writing lead to change? I really don't know. I've long thought it a mystery how the act of writing can lead to answers and insights not easily obtained by simply thinking or even talking about things. I have long believed that the answers lie within and journaling is the vehicle to get there. Beyond that I can say that what was particularly helpful was that we were to write consecutively on the same topic with specific instructions guiding the process. It seemed like with each write I uncovered a new layer of insight, another layer of my personal truth. This helped me challenge old beliefs. Not just challenge them, but to realize that I've made an unfathomable number of choices over the years—choices based on things I no longer believe, want, or need in my life. And with that came the awareness that I can make new choices.

Only one participant's feeling words were lower at the end of the last write (score of 7, somewhat disempowering) than at the start of the first write (score of 11, somewhat empowering). Participant Sixteen was dating a man who represented, for her, an emotionally slippery slope.

Write 1. Starting words: Frustration, understanding, love. *Reflection:* What a mess. I can't sort out this situation because it can't be sorted. I'm in an untenable situation that I have created. On this subject, I have no safety net. . . . I don't want to choose what's best for myself. I thought I was okay with this situation, but now I find I'm really not. *Ending words:* Discomfort, dissatisfaction, hopelessness.

Write 2. Starting words: Calm, restless, satisfied. *Reflection:* This was more narrative this time, fewer feelings, less introspection. I am less emotional than I was with the last write, less wrapped in angst . . . I want so much from this relationship that will never be, so a roller coaster ride is the result. I can get off any time I want. I just don't want to yet. *Ending words:* Uneasy, okay, resigned.

Write 3. Starting words: Happy, content, wondering. *Reflection:* There was little emotion in this write, but satisfaction in what came out. It helped me continue to evaluate this relationship and put it in perspective. This relationship is complicated and a secret from most people, so it's good to put my thoughts and feelings down in writing. It's the only way I can figure it out, it seems. *Ending words:* Satisfied, tired, okay.

Write 4. Starting words: Restless, longing, dissatisfied. *Reflection:* Oh, what a tangled web we weave when first we practice to deceive. I am a little despondent tonight, not for any reason but that I didn't get what I wanted. This write described my restlessness and dissatisfaction with this relationship. It didn't resolve anything or give me any insights. It's reiteration from what I've thought, written, and felt for the last several months. It keeps weaving through my life like a tangled web. Sometimes I think something magic will happen. What I want is a neat, tidy resolution that will leave me unscathed. I have some fear about what will come eventually. *Ending words:* Restless, resigned, dissatisfied.

Participant Sixteen's admission that she "[doesn't] want to choose what's best" for herself offers immediate, if uncomfortable, insight. This is confirmed when she steps back and makes the same interpretation—"I can get off [this roller-coaster ride] any time I want. I just don't want to yet"—from a cognitive, analytic place. The next reflection mediates the first two by balancing introspection, cognition, and emotion, which makes the rawness of the last reflection even starker by comparison. There, we see denial unmasked.

Participant Sixteen is staring straight into the pain. At the two-week follow-up, she wrote:

> Life goes on even when we're being stupid. I am basking in love, and that's all that matters. I am flushed with emotion and wanting to maintain the highs that come with being in love. I don't want to rock this particular boat, I think. But my mind says to move on. I will give time to other pursuits and see where they take me. Maybe I'll learn that I'm okay how I am, that I'll eventually get over this infatuation and become the woman I want to be. There is something to be said for living in the moment, but this moment probably isn't the best one I can have.

Reflection Themes

Not unexpectedly, the themes of the reflections mirrored the instructions for the writes. Reflections from Write #1, which instructed to "tell the story, and include both facts and feelings," focused on emotional and somatic arousal. Several indicated that the "everyday normal" problem they had chosen to write about was perhaps more significant than they had previously let themselves see. Write #2, which focused on layers, details, and context, yielded reflections that demonstrated cognitive appraisal as a primary theme. Several reflections challenged old thought patterns, beliefs, or assumptions. Write #3 asked for meaning. The reflections demonstrated integration of feeling and cognition with resultant insight, along with movement toward self-reliance and self-determination. Write #4 asked for synthesis and an action plan. The reflections demonstrated potential or actual change in cognition, recognition, insight, and/or action.

Following are six excerpts for each write that illustrate the reflections. With the exceptions of Participants Four, Fifteen, and Sixteen, whose reflections have been presented in more detail, the twenty-four reflections below were drawn from all participants.

Reflection # 1 (Emotional and somatic arousal)
I feel relieved but also fear and anxiety, like I opened a whole can of worms.

I am not comfortable looking at this topic, emotionally or physically. At first I noticed a lump in my throat as I wrote, as if I were nervous about speaking out loud.

I can feel in my body (heart rate up a bit, stomach a little jumpy) that this is a very big issue . . . Emotionally, I'm a combination of happy anticipation and nervousness about digging into this issue.

As I wrote I became even more frustrated, which then turned to sadness, even hopelessness. It actually causes my stomach to hurt, to be tied up in knots, unlike anything I have ever noticed before.

Once I sat at the keyboard to do [the first write], I felt unenthusiastic, even with a small tinge of dread. I suddenly didn't want to do this at all.

I'm sensing a tendency to detach from the emotion of all this. To back away from getting too emotionally involved to avoid feeling the disappointment that it seems will come whatever choice I make.

Reflection #2 (Challenging thoughts, beliefs, assumptions)
This walk down memory lane to some of the roots of [topic] is proving valuable. I can see that some of my beliefs are a cop-out. If I believe them, then I don't have to stick my neck out and ask for more—and risk being rejected.

Okay, it appears now that the main thing getting in the way of making a decision isn't so much the issue itself, but that there are two sets of issues. I can feel these two issues fighting for my attention . . . They're mixed up together, but getting in the way of my clear thinking and decision making. Who knew this was so complicated.

It's always a delight to discover what my brain wants to do . . . I've come to trust my brain. It's taken long enough! Ideas may seem way off base or a bit too weird, but eventually, the brain brings them full circle and there's a really cool feeling of that discovery.

I started out being really annoyed with [spouse] but as I wrote, came to the realization of the larger context—that he's worried about finances, can't see any easy solution in sight, certainly not adding more work. Also realized that he doesn't feel good physically . . . The writing was a release for how I'm feeling... but it also helped me to look at the bigger picture/ context of teamwork.

I came to realize that this is a case of having no control and it drives me nuts with catastrophe thinking. Getting the catastrophic thoughts out of my head made space for loving thoughts that I think will help all concerned.

In this writing I did not put as much feeling into it. Instead I wrote "facts," described events. It was not as effective as the last write but it came about because the last write really caused me to reflect on my relationship with my daughter.

Reflection #3 (Integration of thought/feeling, resulting in insight)
The question about the "new normal" was really revelatory for me, because I realized that creating the new normal, or any normal for that matter, has to be normal for *me*. It was freeing to realize that my normal is being true to myself, and I don't need either to emulate anyone else or to think that because I am unlike them, I am not normal. Knowing [this] . . . was a wonderful insight.

What I notice immediately is clarity and a certain amount of bewilderment as to why it has taken so long to get to this place. . . . I'm actually inspired and feel far less fear than I had. . . . I wish I would've had this clarity twenty years ago!

As I wrote this I realized how my internal state reflects my external one. The experiences of the past few years have left me distrustful and have closed me. . . . This was an "aha" moment for me.

I am in a new place, a new depth of understanding. It is not better or worse. It is different. I feel curious and slightly fearful. I suspect I will not like what is revealed here, but it is necessary to keep going. I calm myself and continue. I am not a quitter.

There was a sense of growing strength, a settling in to a new belief. My mind is still preaching caution, but underneath, in my heart, I'm feeling more eager.

This write was like I threw everything out and started over or threw my old story into the air to see what new story would come together when they fell back to earth. Strange.

Reflection #4 (Potential or actual change; action orientation)
I feel liberated this morning. I have defined my new course.

I have somehow learned to transfer some of what I tend to give to others to myself. It seems that I have finally gotten on my own priority list. One obvious action step is to continue to fully engage in [topic], knowing that it is time for me to do so. I have paid my dues and now I can do what I please.

The insight I have gained is the reassurance that I can be at home anywhere.

During the first three writes, I felt sometimes like I was drowning in confusion, rather than floating along a flowing thought-stream that was getting me somewhere. So it was interesting to reread everything and realize not only did it make sense, but several themes were repeating themselves, as if calling my attention to them. . . . What was surprising was the cohesion . . . I did unearth other layers of meaning and essence, and I saw a plan emerge for achieving what I want and need to do.

This has been a powerful way to peel off layers of obfuscation and find myself underneath. My focus has moved an entirely different (and more productive) direction. I feel like I can let go of the surface issue for now. This new understanding will change how I view a lot more than just this one issue.

It seemed like the insight was that any subject, even "everyday normal," can be a window into so much of the Self. Something seemingly mundane and ordinary can hold the extraordinary and even sacred.

In the earliest studies, Pennebaker and Beall (1986) and other colleagues (1990) noted the remarkable insight that participants demonstrated when asked to reflect on the process of writing. LIWC analyses consistently reveal layers of insight and understanding that are implicit in the essays themselves. The reflection write articulates this insight and makes cognitive, affective, and behavioral change more accessible.

Conclusion

Across three decades, social science research confirms that there are physical and mental health benefits to writing deeply about lived or projected experience. The same thirty years has brought to the mainstream American culture an acceptance and normalization for the practice of keeping journals, or writing personal essays, poetry, or memoirs, as tools for personal growth, life management, and creative expression.

The classic research model, adapted for "everyday normal" problems, is a simple, effective, inexpensive, and easily mastered tool.

Thirty years ago, when expressive writing was in its infancy, yoga classes were not available in every hospital, gym, senior center, and adult education program. Today, yoga has become a mainstream option for wellness. What if expressive writing were just as widespread? What if every community in the United States had trained, credentialed facilitators who specialized in helping people write their stories in theoretically solid and experientially effective ways? What might the possibilities be for healthier, happier, higher-functioning individuals, families, workplaces, communities, and societies?

The applications for health, education, welfare, mood stability, problem-solving capacity, and action orientation are vast. Our troubled world needs insight-oriented, solution-focused, self-reliant citizens. Written expression and reflection are accessible and effective tools to help us realize a new paradigm in personal and collective transformation.

References

Adams, Kathleen. 2006. *Journal therapy: Writing as a therapeutic tool: A training workbook*. Brentwood, TN: Cross Country Education.

Burton, Chad M., and Laura A. King. 2004. The health benefits of writing about intensely positive experiences. *Journal of Research in Personality* 38 (2): 150–63.

Chapman, Joyce. 1992. Plenary presentation. 2nd Journal Conference. San Diego: JADE.

Chung, Cindy K., and James W. Pennebaker. 2008. Variations in the spacing of expressive writing sessions. *British Journal of Health Psychology* 13: 15–21.

Frattaroli, Joanne. 2006. Experimental disclosure and its moderators: A meta-analysis. *Psychological Bulletin* 132 (6): 823–65.

Greenberg, Melanie A., Camille B. Wortman, and Arthur A. Stone. 1996. Emotional expression and physical health: Revising traumatic memories or fostering self-regulation? *Journal of Personality and Social Psychology* 71 (3): 588–602.

King, Laura A. 2001. The health benefits of writing about life goals. *Personality and Social Psychology Bulletin* 27 (7): 798–807.

———. 2002. Gain without pain: Expressive writing and self-regulation. In *The writing cure: How expressive writing promotes health and emotional well-being*. S. Lepore and J. Smyth, eds. Washington, DC: American Psychological Association.

King, Laura A., and Kathi N. Miner. 2000. Writing about the perceived benefits of traumatic events: Implications for physical health. *Personality and Social Psychology Bulletin* 26 (2): 220–30.

Pennebaker, James W. 1989. Confession, inhibition and disease. *Advances in Experimental Social Psychology* 22: 211–44.

———. 2000. Telling stories: The health benefits of narrative. *Literature and Medicine* 19 (1): 3–18.

———. 2004. *Writing to heal: A guided journal for recovering from trauma and emotional upheaval*. Oakland, CA: New Harbinger Publications.

Pennebaker, James W., and Sandra K. Beall. 1986. Confronting a traumatic event: Toward an understanding of inhibition and disease. *Journal of Abnormal Psychology* 95 (3): 274–81.

Pennebaker, James W., Michelle Colder, and Lisa K. Sharp. 1990. Accelerating the coping process. *Journal of Personality and Social Psychology* 58 (3): 528–37.

Pennebaker, James W., and Martha E. Francis. 1996. Cognitive, emotional, and language processes in disclosure. *Cognition and Emotion* 10: 601–26.

Pennebaker, James W., and Janel D. Seagal. 1999. Forming a story: The health benefits of narrative. *Journal of Clinical Psychology* 55 (10): 1243–54.

Poon, Alvin, and Sharon Danoff-Burg. 2011. Mindfulness as a moderator in expressive writing. *Journal of Clinical Psychology* 67 (9): 881–95.

Smyth, Joshua M. 1998. Written emotional expression: Effect sizes, outcome types, and moderating variables. *Journal of Consulting and Clinical Psychology* 66 (1): 174–84.

Notes

1. With some nuances of distinction, expressive writing and therapeutic writing are essentially the same. Journal therapy, poetry therapy, interactive bibliotherapy, and memoir/life story each use components of expressive/therapeutic writing. One distinction is that expressive writing (as the term is used outside of the research model) is not necessarily associated with a *therapeutic* intervention; it is often used in community settings, classrooms, support groups, or/and creative writing groups, and autonomously for self-regulation and holistic self-care.

2. The process that I call *reflection writes* was inspired by Joyce Chapman's "feedback statements" (1992).

3. In the research model, *expressive writing* generally refers to the disclosure or release of emotions, traumatic memories, secrets, and other disempowering thoughts and feelings.

4. The time interval between writes does not appear to be a moderator. A meta-analysis by Frattaroli (2006) did not find a difference in effects as a function of the spacing of writing sessions when intervals between writes were longer than twenty-four hours. A study by Chung and Pennebaker (2008) determined that shortened intervals (completing one write per hour for three hours, or even three writes in one hour) "is as effective as the traditional once-per-day approach" (16).

5. "Two strong conclusions can be made with regard to the benefits of writing. First, expressive writing has health benefits. Second, no one really knows why" (King 2002, 119).

6. The study design would not meet institutional research standards. The intent of the study was to provide real-life illustrations of the possibilities inherent when people struggling with day-to-day ("everyday normal") life issues use the research protocol in a structured and purposeful way.

2

Finding Your Shoobeedoo

ROBB JACKSON

When I was a child I lived in a little resort town along Lake Erie in Ohio, the youngest of four. My eldest sibling is fourteen years older than me. After he came home from work on late summer afternoons, he would pile me into his shiny, new 1956 blue-and-white-finned Ford Fairlane with glasspack mufflers and fuzzy dice dangling from the rearview mirror. We'd head to the Pied Piper, the local drive-in ice cream stand, where he'd buy me a nickel cone while he checked out the girls and talked to his friends. Then we'd ride around in his car, the AM radio playing the pop music of this era—a lead voice, male or female, singing its heart out over the background singers' shoobeedoo, shoobeedoo, their accompaniment as regular as a heartbeat while stories of teenage love and angst soared out over the beat.

We humans come fully languaged, or at least with the innate ability to pick up whatever those around us speak, mostly without effort. If we function within normal parameters, we come to understand our relationships with the worlds of our experience, inner and outer, with others, our own selves, and the phenomenal and spiritual worlds around us by means of our language—the one given to us by our particular people, the ones who raised us. We're like linguistic sponges until puberty, learning as native speakers all the nuances of the language used in the world of our experience. Once that language takes root fully in us, we see at least in part through the lens of its peculiarities.

Many scholars have spent their lives trying to understand and to explain these processes. I'm one of them. As a seeker, a sometime poet, a learner, and a teacher, I've stitched together my way of understanding as I've traversed the landscape of my life, and especially as I've tried to midwife others with similar inclinations. For me, everything starts with my inheritance and gift as a human being—what I call my *shoobeedoo*.

This *shoobeedoo* stands as the verbal stream of consciousness that has accompanied my entire life, alive or asleep, as it flows over the rhythm of my heartbeat, my breathing, and the motion or stillness of my body. This wellspring of living language has fed my speaking and eventually, with patient training and determination, my writing.

As I matured, I fed this stream with new words as I listened to the stories of my elders, my parents and siblings, and my teachers. I learned how to decipher the voices of other people by my reading. I learned that there were languages other than my own. My mother didn't learn to speak English until she went to school, and all her family spoke other languages that I could not understand, though I could hear their beauty. Some of my friends' grandparents spoke languages different from my grandparents as well.

As I gained the power to read, I learned to see a library as the collected voices of those who have lived throughout all the human ages. I could borrow these voices and bring them home to speak to me of what they had learned and experienced. In college, I experimented with learning the languages of people who spoke other tongues in other parts of the world.

The world of languages is wide and diverse, and it stretched my imagination as I strived to gather understanding—one planet, many places, and many people with families of languages that lived with their speakers.

By the time I tried to write my own words suitable to print, I knew I wanted to try to teach others to do the same with their words. I've shared my own understanding of how the *shoobeedoo* functions expressively with writing students, both at university and in the community, for the last thirty years.

William Stafford

The issue for me to solve as a teacher was to find a way to make a process I knew for myself, and had witnessed in others, explicit to people who *don't want* to write but *must* write because school requires it. I began by rewinding all the way to my MFA program, where I had the opportunity to study with the poet William Stafford. His journal-based approach to writing poetry impressed me, particularly little gems such as this one:

> A writer is not so much someone who has something to say as he is someone who has found a process that will bring about new things he would not have thought of if he had not started to say them. That is, he does not draw on a reservoir; instead, he engages in an activity that brings to him a whole succession of unforeseen stories, poems, essays, plays, laws, philosophies, religions. (Stafford 1978, 17)

Stafford talks about "receptivity" as he describes the writing process: "To get started I will accept anything that occurs to me. Something always occurs, of course, to any of us. We can't keep from thinking . . . No one else can guide me. I must follow my own weak, wandering, diffident impulses" (17–18).

To get started, Stafford says, we can write anything that occurs to us. Anything? But what if it isn't any good?

> I resolutely disregard these [questions]. Something better, greater, is happening! I am following a process that leads so wildly and originally into new territory that no judgment can at the moment be made about values, significance, and so on. I am making something new, something that has not been judged before. Later others—and maybe I myself—will make judgments. Now, I am headlong to discover. Any distraction may harm the creating. (18)

If this isn't expressive, I don't know what is! We just start writing and give ourselves permission to write anything that occurs to us. Is that it? How does that work? Stafford has an answer to that concern as well: "I know that back of my activity there will be the coherence of my self, and that indulgence of my impulses will bring recurrent patterns and meanings again" (19).

Stafford is sharing what the process is and how it works, the tricks of the trade every student of writing wants to know. But aren't writers, and all artists, supremely talented people with skills that we don't have? He bashes that one, too:

> Without denying that I do have experience, wide reading, automatic orthodoxies, and maneuvers of various kinds, I still must insist that I am often baffled

about what "skill" has to do with the precious little area of confusion when I do not know what I am going to say and then I find out what I am going to say. . . . Skill? If so, it is the skill we all have, something we must have learned before the age of three or four. A writer is one who has become accustomed to trusting that grace, or luck, or—skill. (19)

That "skill" that three-year-olds have is playfulness, a willingness to just do it to see what happens. Unlike a small child, once the writer has found something interesting or important through using this expressive process, he can rewrite and rework the material into a form that will please others who will read it. Revision is the part of writing that is true "work," as any writer will attest, and it comes later. Stafford teaches that anyone who wants to write can write.

James Moffett, William James, Jean Piaget, and Lev Vygotsky

My search led me next to William James, as recollected though James Moffett, who in turn led me to Lev Vygotsky, who handed me my *shoobeedoo*!

James is famous for coining the term *stream of consciousness* (1892), an idea that struck me deeply as I examined my own life. The stream takes many forms: a tumult of words, images, sensory impressions, sounds, memories, shapes, movements, and colors. I realized that I could learn to verbalize this stream with practice, and I concentrated on writing my own experiences with and responses to the never-ending stream within. I wanted to concentrate on the writing part of the stream as it works its way out in my own life. Moffett (1988) brought me back to reconsider the stream of consciousness in this way:

Whatever eventuates as a piece of writing can begin only as some focusing on, narrowing of, tapping off of, and editing of that great ongoing inner panorama that William James dubbed the "stream of consciousness." What I will call here "inner speech" is a version of that stream which has been more verbally distilled and which can hence more directly serve as the wellspring of writing. (Moffett 1988, 91)

As a child grows and develops, normally she will start making sounds that are eventually shaped into what the groundbreaking developmental psychologist Piaget called "egocentric speech," which Moffett describes as

> play prattle (often to objects), "task mediation," or guiding and planning talk accompanying an activity, self-reminders, and just a kind of rehearsing of verbal powers in the form of running observations cued by ongoing or surrounding stimuli. Speech that is egocentric does not distinguish speaker from listener or speaker from subject, in keeping with the general trend of cognitive development to begin in syncretism and move toward discrimination. (93)

Egocentric speech, then, is typified by the babble of small children that accompanies play. As the child continues to develop, language flows along with his activities in a very unselfconscious way. As the still preschool-aged child matures, this language becomes more sophisticated and often mirrors the larger social world of the child. When Piaget observed his own children, he noticed that the incidences of egocentric speech dropped off as the child first entered school. He hypothesized that it had served its cognitive purpose and simply disappeared. I surreptitiously studied my daughter at this age. If I was caught observing her egocentric speech, it stopped altogether, or she turned it into performance.

Vygotsky, a Russian contemporary of Piaget in child development, believed that what Piaget called "egocentric speech" didn't disappear, but it turned inward, becoming inner speech.

> As the child realizes that some speech is really for himself, he deflects it inward. Momentous indeed is this shift from thinking out loud to thinking silently, for the inner life that was constantly manifesting itself in external speech as well as action now becomes inaudible and invisible (expressive body action becoming more subdued also), so that henceforward we cannot regard the child as an open book but must expect him to manifest his mind by excerpting and editing his inner speech. (Moffett 1988, 93)

When all of this is put together, the amazing, generative power of inner speech takes shape. "Inner speech distills not just the stream but a confluence of streams issuing from sensory receptors, memory, and a variety of more or less emotional or logical kinds of reflection. All the elements of this rich mixture trigger, interrupt, and reinforce each other" (92). As children grow, they are taught instead to "give the teacher what she wants" so that they may score high grades. This makes the teacher the arguable "author" of their writing, since students must "get it right." Students see writing as a mimicking of an adult authority figure's voice, which makes it boring. This is why so many of my students find it liberating to rediscover their early childhood inner speech, although most of them have absolutely no idea of how to harness its force as a tool to create a written voice on the page.

Moffett pulls this all together in one fell swoop: "However personal or impersonal the subject matter, all writing as authoring must be some revision of inner speech for a purpose and an audience" (96).

The Shoobeedoo Model of Expressive Writing

What do we need to get started writing? Humans from eight to eighty will usually answer "a pen and paper" or "a computer." Another good response is "a brain." The brain is the locus of self, and the mind is what the brain does. The stream of consciousness seems to flow through our inner world, the world of our mind. There are various sources of input and stimulation that affect the flow.

First, there is *sensory stimulation*—touch, smell, taste, sight, sound. Our senses bring the world outside us to our minds in palatable ways.

Memories are complexes of sensory stimulation, with associated feeling states, that are stored in our brains. Memories can be triggered in many different ways, including sensory stimulation. A particular sound or smell can evoke a powerful memory spontaneously.

What is *spiritual* is often intuited, but for many people it has a voice that must be distinguished from one's own inner speech. Wisdom begins with discernment. Which internal "voice" is which? We may hear a parental voice when the conscience perks up, and then there is our own legitimate thought-voice. In addition, we learn over time to discern the "gentle whisper" (1 Kings 19:12, NIV) that many may call simply Spirit.

These various substreams in the larger stream of consciousness can trigger each other spontaneously and in myriad ways, all of which can be verbalized through our inner speech (brain talk, thought voice, *shoobeedoo*). When we are in a calm and peaceful state, it is possible to witness our moment-to-moment life as a flickering series of inner and outer thoughts and experiences, forward and backward in time—a flowing tumble triggered externally by sensory stimulation and/or internally by memory in a thousand flitting, incalculable intersections, burbling along moment by moment.

The Chooser

A "chooser" accompanies our inner speech. We can choose to make inner speech available via outer speech or talking. To do this spontaneously and in a sustained fashion requires a kind of verbal fluency and a mother tongue. Or we might instead choose to route inner speech into writing on paper or typing on a keyboard, both of which require another kind of manual dexterity, coupled with an intuitive grasp of the symbol system of a language.

A Shoobeedoo Demonstration: How Filters Get Installed

Learning about one's *shoobeedoo* is a hazardous venture that I'll illustrate with a story. My British wife and I were fresh off the plane from visiting her family. She's the designated driver in England, as I'm not good at navigating the opposites. On our way home from the airport, we stopped at the supermarket. I was steering the shopping cart, so my *shoobeedoo* started flashing on the relationship of driving cars in England and shopping carts in America while we trudged through the store.

While I was musing on the driving styles of the other shoppers, I noticed one young woman who appeared to be pregnant. She wore a loose-fitting floral muumuu and bright pink flip-flops. In her basket, in the child strap-down seat, was a diapered baby of indeterminate gender. On the floor was a little boy about three, very confident as he used his egocentric speech by chattering about this and that, while his mother gathered her groceries in the crowd of shoppers.

A large woman streamed down the aisle toward us. She was older than the young mother, though she, too, wore a muumuu and bright flip-flops. She was enormous but definitely not pregnant.

Right at that moment, the little boy looked up, and bellowed out, "Mommy! Look at the fat lady!" What happened next was predictable, at least in this part of the world. The little boy's mommy smacked him on the bottom repeatedly until he cried, the amount of pain inflicted calculated to the exact point of the dishonor of the oncoming woman. She showed all of us that she didn't teach her kid to trash talk heavyset ladies in grocery stores!

I've thought about this incident many times since it happened, and I've shared the story with many groups of people who have helped me deconstruct the event with regard to the functioning of one's *shoobeedoo*. The little boy saw the large woman, the sensory experience activated his inner speech, and, lickety-split, the inner speech shot out his mouth into outer speech and thus into the world at large. It happened so fast there was no stopping it. The child hadn't yet learned about the power of his chooser. He saw that lady, his face raised up, and his little arm pointed at her directly as he shouted out his discovery in something like sheer wonder and amazement.

There's an inherent injustice in the story's outcome familiar to us all. Yes, the oncoming lady was fat. The little boy spoke the truth. Why did he suffer so for saying something we all could verify if we were honest? Did the oncoming lady really think the young mother taught her son to say such things? Not likely. Once, after reflecting on my story, another woman told me, "I bet he heard his daddy teasing his momma about being pregnant, and the little boy was actually mimicking his father in pointing out another pregnant lady to his momma!" Could be. If this interpretation is true, then what the little boy shouted was more of an affirmation of affiliation. Why then did the child get spanked? For the social honor of the offended lady. Life is like this, and it often has deleterious effects upon the development of one's *shoobeedoo*.

Here is where pain fits into the model. We learn not to say everything we hear in our heads, and pain is the teacher. Whether it's physical pain (a beating), verbal pain (ridicule), social pain (the shame of a bad grade), or a humiliating combination (getting spanked in front of a supermarket full of people), we generally learn to stuff our genuine thoughts and feelings. In abusive environments, children can learn even to disavow or stifle inner speech altogether and later must be taught by mentors how to find it and express it again safely. Pain creates a filter and awakens the chooser.

Far too often, almost universally, this filter gets installed on writing in school as well. Generally speaking, school teaches students to be fearful of writing. Those of us who do like to write probably started before we went to school, or we had a special mentor/teacher who permitted us the delights of real writing. Since fluency building, both in writing and speaking, is so important for learning purposes, it stands to reason that writers must learn to be aware of their own filters and ultimately the painful narratives that first installed them, and with patience and determination learn to overcome them in order to become fluent writers who can instantaneously route the resources of their inner speech and inner life onto the page. This characteristic fluency is, after all, what creates one's written voice.

> What really teaches composition—"putting together"—is disorder. Clarity and objectivity become learning challenges only when content and form are *not* given to the learner but when he must find and forge his own from his inchoate thought. (Moffett 1988, 96)

This kind of real compositing from the *shoobeedoo* requires a certain self-confidence, permission, and sense of authority from the writer that isn't often conferred on students. I suppose this is why so many of us have come to writing in the first place through journaling and other forms of private self-expression. From here, too, probably stems our culture's view that writers are unusually talented or gifted. Stafford and Moffett say, and I agree, "No, that's simply not true."

Rhetorical Constraints on Expressive Writing

At this point, many students start gathering the wrong idea about the role of the *shoobeedoo* in writing. They tend to see it as "anything goes," in an anarchic sense. While it is true that many writers find a sort of bliss in the raw flow of free expression in their notebooks and journals, they also use language to impose an order and structure on inchoate thought. Early on, I use the *shoobeedoo* to discover what I really mean, but that raw material must usually be rewritten if someone else is to read it and make sense of it. Herein lies the importance of the processes of writing, a sort of procedural knowledge. After the initial discovery (the *aha!*) comes revision and rewriting. First we develop fluency in writing, then clarity, and maybe, ultimately, correctness. It seldom works the other way around.

This is where the "rhetorical constraints" fit into expressive approaches to writing. We must understand how rhetorical forces work to constrain the *shoobeedoo* for the purposes of communication with other people outside us. These rhetorical constraints can be author centered or audience/reader centered. They can relate to purpose, meaning/content/message, context, or text form/genre.

Perhaps it is useful to sketch out how these constraints work in our writing. In journal writing, the *author* is the self, the person writing. The *purpose* is determined by the author as well, and that purpose can take many different forms. It could be to find out where I am in my life, to explore fears or hopes or desires, or to simply express anger or fear or concern. The *audience* is myself. No one will see what I write unless I decide to share it later; right now, I am writing for myself alone. The *meaning* is self-driven and self-derived as well, and the *context* may be my easy chair in my living room where I'm listening to music, or my writing station where I'm peering out the window. Journal writing may be its own *text form* (or *genre*), but it might also use other genres such as poetry, fiction, nonfiction, and drama, as well. Many journal writers see their journals as a special kind of place where they first create and then later find deposits of precious ores, metals, and diamonds that they may mine to create other, more public, forms.

What is absolutely essential to me (and, I believe, to most journal writers) is that my journal is private. I hold to this principle not because of any particular content that resides in my journal, but more as a formative principle. If I think someone will find what I write and read it, they become an intuited audience and constrain my expression. Only when I feel reasonably safe that no one will see my writing am I free to write whatever I like, following the meandering path laid down by my *shoobeedoo*. With this understanding comes a kind of freedom that is both liberating and essential to expression itself. I can write whatever I like just to see what's on my mind. I can dawdle, experiment, fume, castigate, whatever—just because it's permissible and it pleases me. By testing possibilities I find out what I really mean by seeing it on the page. Equally, I can recognize ideas that occur to me but really don't quite work as mine.

How an individual writer conceptualizes a journal, commonplace book, or sketchbook is up to the individual, but having one is essential to any writer. A journal becomes a repository for inner speech and a vital tool for finding and honoring one's own *shoobeedoo*. Understanding how rhetorical forces constrain expressive writing can actually free one up in important ways. At the journal stage, writing for myself alone, I can use techniques that stimulate my *shoobeedoo* to flow freely. According to Stafford (1978), writers' "'creations' come about through confident reliance on stray impulses that will, with trust, find occasional patterns that are satisfying" (20). Later, when mining my journal for bits useful to others, I might reshape that material for a public audience of readers by using another genre—poetry, or an essay (prose nonfiction), or a short story (prose fiction)—for an entirely different purpose. Understanding the interplay of the *shoobeedoo* and rhetorical constraints, we "have the whole unexplored realm of human vision" (20) at our fingertips.

Writing Light into Darkness

Upon further reflection, the "why" of expressive writing, its potential social and spiritual role, rises up. Not only do I have a *shoobeedoo*, so does everyone else, creating a great democratizing of us all on this planet. Everybody can write if they want to, though they must learn the craft: how to find the words, how to bring them to the page, what to do with them once found and placed, how to shape what they bring, how to celebrate and share this capacity with others—first, perhaps, their own loved ones who rejoice in their achievement. They must learn how this writing isn't school and that they can do this out of the sheer joy of doing it.

We can heal, we can learn, we can become better and more fully alive humans, and best of all, it's free—a birthright of all people of any language in any nation, any place, anywhere on earth. Sadly, yes, we "are like God, knowing good and evil" (Genesis 3:5, NIV), but in this one small way we can create something new, something maybe no one else has made, which connects us to everyone else who has ever lived.

We write as individuals, but often in "camps," little groups of people drawn together for a time to celebrate and encourage each other. We make new things, together rejoicing and sharing. Although it involves self, it's really not about self. It's about casting antennae into the ether of space with others who are doing the same. We've come together to do this now for a number of possible reasons. The most important thing is that we've come together. Our collections, our books, are testimonies of our gathering together, a way to share with others who can read what we found when we gathered to listen. Ultimately, we must learn how to make ourselves available to Spirit—through our *shoobeedoo*—if we are to thrive together as people on one planet.

References

International Bible Society. 1984. *The holy Bible: New international version* (NIV). Grand Rapids, MI: Zondervan Publishing House.

James, William. 1892. A stream of consciousness. In *Classics in the history of psychology*. Christopher D. Green, ed. Toronto: York University, http:// psychclassics.yorku.ca/James/jimmy11.htm.

Moffett, James. 1988. Writing, inner speech, and meditation. In *Coming on center: Essays in English education*, 2nd ed. Portsmouth, NH: Heinemann.

Stafford, William. 1978. A way of writing. In *Writing the Australian crawl: Views on the writer's vocation*. Ann Arbor, MI: University of Michigan Publishing.

3

The Journal Ladder[1]

KATHLEEN ADAMS

In the nearly thirty years that I have immersed myself in the field of expressive and therapeutic writing, I have watched it evolve from the seed of a concept into a vigorous tree bearing fruits of healing and change for so many who pick up the pen and write.

My first venture into the field was the creation of a twelve-hour course on journal writing, now known as the Journal to the Self® workshop. The earliest offering introduced the structure of discrete journal techniques as a principal organizing feature. There were twenty-one writing techniques in the early days, each with its own inherent properties, qualities, and reasonably reliable outcomes. The techniques ranged from fast writing sprints that might only take five minutes to a structured written conversation that might take two hours or more.

The techniques are like tools in a toolbox. Just as a hammer is the right choice for placing a nail in the wall, so a particular journal technique or device might be exactly the right tool to achieve a particular desired outcome, such as expressing anger, exploring conflicting thoughts, moderating a disagreement with a colleague, or capturing moments of joy (Adams 1990).

For example, a popular and timeless journal technique is the unsent letter. This is a journal entry that follows the conventional form of a letter—a salutation to the addressee, followed by a message from the writer's point of view that may share news, express feelings or opinions, make requests, or invite response. The difference is that an unsent letter is written with the knowledge and intention that it will not actually be sent or shared. Benefits include the freedom to fully express without need for explanation or restraint; one can be as socially inappropriate as one wishes, with no negative consequences. Unsent letters also offer the opportunity to articulate what has been unspoken. The unsent letter technique is often used when there are hurt feelings, misunderstandings, or anger between the writer and someone else. The technique is also excellent for expressing grief or loneliness. Unsent letters often bring an immediate sense of release and relief.

Perhaps the most commonly used technique is *free writing* (sometimes called *stream of consciousness writing* or *flow writing*). This is the default technique of nearly every journal writer. It is simplicity personified: Put pen to page, or fingers to keyboard, and write spontaneously, without forethought of where the writing might go, what might be discovered, how long it might take, or even if there will be outcomes.

Structure, Pacing, Containment

Fairly early in my clinical practice, I was tasked with creating a journal therapy program for clients who experienced difficulties writing. There are many skill levels and cognitive and emotional styles, and one technique—even one as versatile as free writing—doesn't address them all.

By its very nature, free writing is free from any defined structure. It is also free from containment. There are no limits; it can take minutes or hours, paragraphs or pages. There is no organic or intentional pacing. It might skim along the surface, bright but shallow, or it might plunge into the darkest depths.

Under several sets of circumstances, free writing is simply *not* the best choice. Some writers have traumatic histories, and the unstructured style of free writing may bring with it vivid, unpleasant, uncontained memories of abuse or crisis. Other writers prefer more order and better limits. "Leftbrained" writers, who rely on information more than intuition, often report that free writing is too ambiguous and unreliable. Writers with limited attention spans, learning disabilities, limited literacy skills, or cognitive or motor skill impairment frequently cannot sustain free writing for long enough time intervals to produce useful outcomes.

Recognizing the inherent lack of structure, pacing, and containment that free writing represents, and faced with the challenge of finding a method for writers at all levels and learning styles, I placed free writing at one end of a continuum and considered: What's at the other end? What is the most structured, paced, contained journal technique of all?

Sentence stems, a technique that requires only the completion of a partially constructed sentence, was the immediate answer:

- *Right now I should . . .*
- *I feel . . .*
- *I wish I knew . . .*
- *Today I am . . .*

Everyone who reads and writes knows the structure of his own language. The pacing of single sentences is straightforward. The container is limited; even complex sentences are only a line or two.

Table 3.1 gives brief descriptions of fourteen techniques in the journal toolbox, all of which appear on the Journal Ladder.

The Journal Ladder

With the filters of structure, pacing, and containment in place, I looked freshly at my toolbox of journal techniques. I assigned them each a place on a continuum that ranged from sentence stems to free writing. The result is a model called the Journal Ladder (Adams 1998). It offers a continuum of journal therapy techniques, starting with the ones that have the most structure, pacing, and containment, and ending with the ones that have the least (figure 3.1).

Clients responded enthusiastically. They were relieved to have a new way of thinking about their journal writing, and they appreciated the many choices available. When they learned how to structure, pace, and contain their writing, they were able to select a technique that matched their mood,

Table 3.1. The Journal Toolbox: Fourteen Writing Techniques on the Journal Ladder (Adapted from Adams 1999)

Technique on ladder, bottom to top	Description
Sentence Stems	A sentence-completion process. Fill in the blank with a word or phrase. May be very universal (Right now I feel . . .) or highly customized to an individual's immediate question, problem, or interest.
Five-Minute Sprint	A timed writing process designed to bring focus and intensity in short bursts. Excellent for those who are resistant or aversive to journal writing, or who are uncertain about how to start, or who state they do not have time to write journals.
Inventory	A problem-solving/goal-setting approach to quickly identify an area of difficulty, the goal or vision for resolution, and a brainstormed list of action steps to take.
Structured Write	A series of sentence stems grouped and sequenced to reveal consistently deepening layers of information and awareness.
Clustering	Visual free-association from a central word or phrase. Lines and circles connect key thoughts and associations to the central core. Work quickly to maximize results. Cluster until a felt-sense shift occurs (usually three to seven minutes, then switch to a five-minute sprint to synthesize findings.
List of 100	A list of one hundred items, many of which will probably be repetitions, on a predetermined theme or topic. Repetition is an important part of the process. Topics can be about any current issue (for example: 100 Things I'm Sad About; 100 Things I Need or Want to Do; 100 Places I Would Like to See). At the end of the list, group the responses into themes or topics and count up entries for each.

(continued on page 47)

time frame, and desired outcome. Clients also discovered along the way that there were a few techniques that they found to be especially helpful, interesting, or enjoyable. They learned to dive deeply with their writing, but then come back to the surface for breath and sunlight.

With the qualities of structure, pacing, and containment guiding their discoveries, clients found that their journals became treasured symbols of new lives made by hand.

Three Sections

Although I originally conceptualized the journal ladder as a tool to measure relative structure, pacing, and containment in a journal technique, there are

Table 3.1. *(continued from page 46)*

Technique on ladder, bottom to top	Description
Alphapoem	Write the alphabet, A–Z, or any collection of letters, vertically down the side of a page. Then write a poem in which each successive line begins with the next letter. Alternatively, use a word or phrase as the poem's spine. Excellent for groups as it promotes a high level of participation and sharing. Adolescents and reluctant writers respond well.
Captured Moments	Vignettes capturing the sensations of a particularly meaningful or emotional experience. Written from the senses with strong descriptors. Captured moments of beauty, joy, blessing, calm can add balance, hope, and perspective to a challenging time.
Unsent Letter	A metaphoric communication to another that is written with the specific intention that it will not be shared.
Character Sketch	A written portrait of another person, an aspect of the self, or an intangible such as an emotion or an obstacle. Describe outward appearance as well as actual or imagined personality characteristics, motivations, fears, needs, desires, etc.
Dialogue	A metaphoric conversation written in two voices. Anyone or anything is an appropriate dialogue partner. There is no constriction by time, space, physical reality, or literal voice (Progoff 2002).
Perspectives	An alteration in point of view that provides a different perspective on an event or situation.
Springboards	A free write with a prompt (question, thought, focus). Otherwise, no structure, pacing, or containment.
Free Writing	Unboundaried, unstructured, unpaced narrative writing. Useful for creative flow or spontaneous writing sessions. Can be structured by adding a time limit or page limit.

two other features worth noting. First, the techniques on the ladder move from the concrete to the abstract. Second, along the concrete/abstract pathway, the techniques first offer information (the "known" of the conscious mind), then reveal insight (the "remembered" of the subconscious mind), and finally access intuitive understanding (the "unknown" of the unconscious mind).

When a writer's emotional and cognitive processing styles were taken into account, a section of the ladder could be chosen that would likely be most helpful, and the techniques in that section could be calibrated to match the writer's presenting problems and desired outcomes.

The Lower Rungs: Structure

The lower third of the ladder—the five techniques from sentence stems to clustering—are by far the most accessible to the largest number of writers,

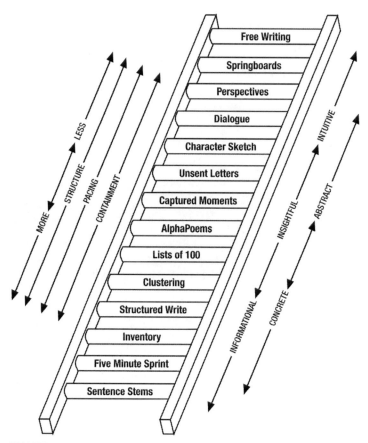

FIGURE 3.1
The Journal Ladder

because they are short, simple, and easy to learn. These techniques can be completed in under fifteen minutes—some in one to five minutes—and their inherent structure appeals to those who are analytically minded, as well as those who have higher levels of reluctance, timidity, or resistance.

The techniques in the lower rungs of the ladder are quite disarming in their simplicity. The five-minute sprint, for instance, is nothing more than a timed writing process, written quickly. The two structuring elements are the container of time and the crisp pacing of keeping the pen moving or the fingers flying across the keys.

It is astonishing how consistently even five scant minutes can reveal ideas, information, and possible solutions. When I teach this technique, I ask writers to keep the pen moving for five minutes about a topic on their minds, regardless of relative significance (e.g., planting the garden or contemplating a major life change have equal validity). When they have finished, writers silently reread what they have written and give themselves a sentence or two of reflection, starting with the sentence stem, *As I read this, I notice . . .* Writers consistently report noticing greater clarity, connection between thoughts and feelings, and possibilities that had been hidden or ignored.

The Middle Rungs: Insight

The techniques that stimulate insight—the revealed patterns, the causal relationships, the sudden flashes of awareness—live in the middle rungs of the journal ladder, from lists of 100 to character sketches. Writers who are motivated to understand themselves or their life events, as well as those who are curious, interested in human relationships, and/or welcoming of change and growth, successfully use these techniques. Of course, anyone whose emotional and cognitive processing styles match the middle rungs of the ladder can also make effective use of the techniques in the lower rungs.

The insight-oriented rungs are characterized by a sense of discovery. It is common for a list of 100 or an alphapoem to elicit information that is out of the realm of the known or expected. The surprise brings curiosity and lightness, and there is more balance in the journal.

Balance is a key component of expressive writing. Many people turn to their journals when life is difficult, when they are emotionally upset, or when there is a crisis or challenge to resolve right away. When the emergency passes, they toss the journal aside and don't write again until there is another difficulty. Certainly there is great benefit from the immediacy and cathartic release of crisis writing. There are also great benefits to adding balance both to the journal and to life by writing about joy, gratitude, harmony, and intimacy. When writers pay attention to small moments of beauty (the moon through clouds, a child's laughter, dinner with a friend), or, at day's end, make short lists of gratitudes, pleasures, or experiences, they usually report feeling surprisingly better, even in the midst of difficulty.

The Upper Rungs: Intuition

By the time we reach the upper rungs of the ladder—from dialogue to free writing—we are working with the techniques that create pathways to the intuitive mind. These techniques penetrate deeply. Perhaps they access the same areas of the unconscious mind that are activated by dreamwork or meditation. Like meditation and dreamwork, the techniques in the upper section often generate symbols, images, archetypes, and abstractions. People who are best suited for these techniques tend to be comfortable with the unseen universe. They often have deeply rooted spiritual pathways and can hold paradox and ambiguity without undue stress. They are cognitively capable of abstract and metaphoric thinking, and they are able to write at depth for extended intervals of time without physical or emotional exhaustion.

Some of the techniques in the ladder's upper section involve the temporary suspension of rational states of consciousness. The dialogue technique comes from the work of Dr. Ira Progoff (2002), a depth psychologist who pioneered the field of journal therapy. It involves a written conversation in which the writer speaks in his/her own voice, then takes on the role and voice of the dialogue partner. The dialogue partner can be anyone or anything at all: a person in the writer's life, an aspect of the self, an inanimate object, a state of health or disease, an abstraction or symbol, or the guidance of inner wisdom. "Man does indeed know intuitively more than he rationally understands," said Progoff, and the dialogue technique is a gateway to the "knowledge beyond understanding that comes to us at depth" (Progoff 1989).

The Journal Ladder has been used to support the treatment goals of those living with post-traumatic stress, disabling illness, mood disorders, the frail elderly, recovering alcoholics, those in grief, and many other life transitions and difficulties. It enhances the satisfaction, pleasure, and positive outcomes for writers who are not struggling with any particular difficulty but write for personal growth and enjoyment. The method is easy to learn and requires very little practice to independently implement. It is a simple and effective structure for any number of expressive writing situations.

References

Adams, Kathleen. 1990. *Journal to the self: Twenty-two paths to personal growth.* New York: Grand Central Publishing (originally Warner Books).

——. 19s98. *The way of the journal: A journal therapy workbook for healing,* 2nd ed. Lutherville, MD: Sidran Press.

——. 1999. Writing as therapy. In *Counseling and Human Development.* Denver: Love Publishing.

——. 2011. Journal therapy as a pathway for healing and growth. *Journal of Humanities Therapy* 2 (12): 69–82.

Progoff, Ira. 1989 (4). Lecture. Intensive Journal Workshop®, Denver, CO.

——. 2002. *At a journal workshop.* Los Angeles: Jeremy Tarcher.

Note

1. Adapted from the author's own work (Adams 2011).

4

Journal Writing in the Counseling Relationship

KATE THOMPSON

Journal writing is gaining recognition and respect as a useful and profoundly helpful tool for clients within the counseling relationship. Journal writing can be useful for the counselor as well; it offers a simple but effective method for self-supervision and reflective practice. This chapter discusses some of the most effective journal techniques for clients and counselors alike. The Journal Ladder (see Adams, chapter 3) provides an ideal model for working with counseling clients where structure, pacing, and containment are vital considerations, given the serious nature of some of the presenting problems clients bring to counseling.

Until 2010 I spent most of my career working as a clinical counselor in the British National Health Service. I worked in the offices of primary care doctors seeing their medical patients.[1] Referrals covered a huge range of issues including depression and anxiety, bereavement, personality disorders, relationship issues, sexuality, and many psychosomatic presentations. My clients were aged sixteen or older. Most often, I was restricted to six to eight sessions with each one. The time-limited nature of the work meant that anything I could do to give my patients support between and beyond our sessions was very desirable.

This often meant introducing therapeutic journal writing techniques. Although not a common intervention, journal therapy (using journals as an adjunct to counseling) proved very useful for many of my clients and provided

Caveat

Simply to invite a client to "write down all your thoughts and feelings" in a journal could be ill-advised. This work is powerful; writing can reach deeply into the unknown and unacknowledged. Writing without appropriate structure, pacing, containment, and/or support may be risky if a client:

- is unstable
- lacks self-awareness
- lacks internal or external resources to cope with surprises and unexpected events
- has or may have a major mental illness
- has fragile ego strength
- has unresolved trauma, whether or not known or disclosed

The Journal Ladder (see Adams, chapter 3) provides an ideal model for working with counseling clients where structure, pacing, and containment are vital considerations.

them with a self-sustaining method of support they could continue to access between sessions and after discharge.

The suggestion that a client write a journal is variously met with confusion, consternation, suspicion, or skepticism. Clients often say that they don't know where to begin or don't understand what the benefit would be. Sometimes they are resistant or don't readily comply.

Often there is work to do in engaging clients in the process. When the task is introduced carefully and clearly—assuring the client that spelling, grammar, and punctuation don't matter, that writing can be done by hand or on a computer, that the goal isn't to write well but to express thoughts and feelings honestly—the client can take small steps forward.

One of the first things I introduce with clients is the concept of the *feedback loop* (Thompson 2004), also known as the reflection write (see Adams, chapter 1), which I encourage with every journal entry. The feedback loop transforms the journal into a therapeutic tool and takes it beyond the simply cathartic, descriptive, or daily record.

The feedback loop involves reading back the journal entry, either silently or aloud, then writing a feedback statement to provide a reflective response to what has been written. This would normally be just a sentence or two, perhaps beginning:

When I read this I notice . . .

When I read this I feel . . .

When I read this I am surprised that . . .

This feedback stage allows people to recognize what they have written, perhaps for the first time. It is the place where journal writing moves from the cathartic to the analytical stage and where learning, insight, and growth can occur. When people see what they have written, it is no longer hidden. It becomes visible, and so do they. As one client said:

When I read this I know I exist—I can see me on the page.

Six Journal Techniques for Counseling Settings

Six journal techniques that consistently produce good results in counseling settings are *lists, steppingstones, captured moments, unsent letters, dialogues,* and *perspectives.*

Lists

Lists are a good place to begin for clients who have not kept journals before or do not have the energy or motivation to write much. Because lists become a way of asserting a measure of control and seeing the emergence of structure, they can be a practical tool for people overwhelmed by chaotic life circumstances. Clients who feel harried or out of control can be encouraged to write a list of "three gratitudes" or "three accomplishments" each day

(Adams 1999). Sometimes clients protest that they can't think of three things to be grateful for, or they don't get three things done in a day. Here's how a conversation might go:

Client: *What do I have to be thankful for? There's nothing in my life that works.*

Counselor: *Well, let's just have a look; even the tiniest thing will count.*

Client: *Like, I wake up? A bird sings?*

Counselor: *Yes, exactly! Can you look for three tiny things each day this week? And write them down?*

Client: *Okay, I'll try it for a week.*

The act of keeping even a short list of achievements is an achievement. Similarly, gratitude lists can introduce notes of hope and beauty in an otherwise monochrome existence. The commitment to a habit this small can be a first step to positive change, such as the self-observation that allows the writer to step outside the engulfing absorption and develop new perspectives.

I encourage clients to keep a list of "Things I Will Not Talk to Kate About." We acknowledge the existence of the list, and periodically we may review it with questions like:

- Are the items on your list still the same?
- Have you added anything?
- Have we talked about anything that you can now cross off the list?

Sometimes people will tell me what's on the list:

- my secret lover
- I was abused
- I used to throw up after dinner every night
- panic attacks

Sometimes this means that we will eventually talk about these things, and sometimes it means that the client will begin to think about them alone. It can be very liberating and permissive not to have to talk about them, but simply to acknowledge their existence.

Steppingstones

A list of life markers, turning points, or other themes, *steppingstones* (Progoff 1992) can be used to follow themes over the life span. There are many different kinds of steppingstone threads that can provide other ways of approaching issues in counseling. The classic steppingstones are life events—beginning with *I was born*. Progoff recommends a list of eight to twelve steppingstones. They can be written in the order in which they come to mind but then read aloud chronologically. Each one may subsequently reward greater scrutiny.

Looking at crossroads, or roads not taken, in the past can help to reassess the life being lived or bring back forgotten ways of being, habits abandoned, or relationships neglected.

The relationship between the past and the present is often illuminated gently and powerfully through writing *landscape steppingstones*, a list of places that have been important, including residences, environments, places visited, and other significant landscapes.

Susan wrote landscape steppingstones and then chose one to explore in depth. It was the landscape of Alabama, on a family trip when she was a child. Her father had been short-tempered on the trip. In the writing, Susan realized how her father had struggled with the segregation between black and white of the late 1950s. She understood for the first time that her father's snappish demeanor was not a result of the children's transgressions but arose from his deep discomfort at the world they were driving through.

Captured Moments

Captured moments (Adams 1990) are short (five- to eight-minute) bursts of experience and intense emotional connection. They are particularly useful in helping clients recapture, remember, restore, and re-story specific moments of existence. This is the technique I am most likely to use within a session, in a face-to-face encounter with experienced and inexperienced journal writers alike. These are existential moments caught on the page.

Nita had been depressed for several months. It was not her first experience with what she called the *grey blanket holding me down, the monochrome world where all the color has leached out.*

I guided her through the first steps: Write in the first person, present tense, using the language of the senses. Then I said:

Let your mind wander back over the day. Notice anything you experienced as having more color, anything other than the monochrome world.

At first her resistance spoke loudly on the page:

There isn't anything. Everything is grey—the weather, the sky, the pavements, the buildings.

But as she wrote, Nita began to notice things. Writing brought things into her conscious mind that she hadn't known she knew. Details returned to her world:

I'm walking to the doctor's office, it's grey, the sky's grey like every day. My feet are heavy, my shoulders weary. I take one heavy step after another. The world around me smells damp and grey. But now I suddenly notice a flower—a yellow flower, a daffodil, green leaves in the grey city street, bright yellow trumpet. I think I know how Wordsworth felt . . .

This is how captured moments can crack open the grey shell to reveal the luminous pearl within. When they are written as a regular practice, they create a sensory string of pearls that can be comforting and inspiring as the client goes forward.

Unsent Letter

Colette said, when one we love dies
there's no reason to stop
writing them letters.

—*Michaels 2000, 185*

Writing *unsent letters*—as the name suggests, letters that stay safely in the journal and thus can hold uncensored expression—is frequently suggested in circumstances of loss or bereavement. Writing an unsent letter can, for some people, start the grieving process. Writing about loss does not have to be restricted to people. A student of mine wrote unsent letters to a house in which she had lived for many years and finally had to sell. She hadn't realized how deeply she was grieving, or that her depression was really about this loss of a significant place.

Danny had been a pot smoker since his midteens. When he and his girlfriend wanted a baby, he decided to quit for health and financial reasons. "I want to become the kind of dad I wish I'd had," he said. Marijuana became *Mari* in this letter, in which he gives her notice that he is moving on:

> *Dear Mari,*
> *You've been my friend for many years. My home has been yours. In the dark times you were there for me, and I'm grateful. At first it was a good game we played—Jim, Carol, me, and Jane. Friends together. Then I remember the times when you took me out of myself, when I think I needed you, when Jane split with me.*
>
> *Your smell, your comforting arms. "Relax, chill," you said. "Nothing can ever be too bad that we can't deal with it." We flew together, with Susie, when she first came. Now she wants you out, too—we need more time for us and she wants, we want to try for a baby.*
>
> *So it's time for you to go. You need to leave me now. It can't go on. I have to do it alone now. I'll always be grateful and know that I invited you in and now I have to tell you to go. After next Friday I can't have you in the house again. That's it.*
> *Sorry mate,*
> *Danny* (Thompson 2011, 190)

His feedback:

> *When I read this I feel like I'm giving notice to an old and dear friend—after eight years together. I feel some sadness but it so feels the right thing to do at this time, and I have a great feeling about the future.*

Adolescent journal writers, from Anne Frank onward, have often personified their journals so that the whole exercise becomes one long, unsent letter. Suggesting this to teenage clients can make the task of writing far less daunting. The journal becomes a friend.

Dialogues

A journal *dialogue* is a written conversation in which the writer assumes both voices (Progoff 1992). On the page, dialogues resemble a film or play script. There are six major types of dialogue referenced in Progoff's work, with many permutations within the general categories. Some common types of dialogue used in counseling include dialogues with:

- individual persons, living or dead or unborn
- anyone or anything lost, grieved, or mourned
- illness, symptom, or physical condition
- parts of the self (subpersonalities), including inner critic, inner coach, inner wisdom
- parts of the body
- qualities or feelings

Helen was an athlete who was prevented from competing in a road race by a nasty fall. She worked through her frustration by writing a dialogue with her body:

Helen: *How are you feeling today?*

Body: *I'm tired and I ache and it's hard.*

Helen: *Well, you should have seen that extra step and not gone over. Now we're stuck here and have to make the best of it.*

Body: *You feel as if I've let you down, don't you?*

Helen: *Oh, a bit, I'm cross and frustrated and I suppose I'm blaming you.*

Body: *You sound like a baby whose candy's been stolen.*

Helen: *That's a bit how I feel; I feel deprived. Running is important to me. I feel so good when we are out there away from it all and feeling strong and healthy. Mostly you support me and give me so much.*

Body: *It won't be long. We have to be patient though and find a way of staying healthy.*

Helen: *So perhaps a bit of gentle yoga will be good for us, not a deprivation after all.*

Body: *I'll give it a try.*

Helen: *Me, too.* (Thompson 2011, 135)

In this exchange, Helen was able to express her frustration as well as deeper feelings of deprivation and loss. She found an encouraging inner voice that supported new thinking, and she used it to find adaptations to feel "strong and healthy" until she could run again. But it wasn't until her reflection that she acknowledged an important barrier to her success:

> When I read this I am really in touch with my frustration and see myself as a bit of an idiot—it wasn't a glamorous fall. I think that stops me from focusing on the things I know are good for me and could help me heal. (Thompson 2011, 135)

Clients who write dialogues with physical illnesses frequently find they develop a new perspective, acceptance, or attitude. Writing a dialogue with diabetes, leukemia, asthma, or another illness can help the client befriend the condition they so resent. Getting to know the illness through metaphoric conversation often leads to increased medication compliance, lifestyle changes, and improvement in health and quality of life.

Writing a dialogue with an illness can peel away defenses and denial. In a dialogue with her breast cancer, Elizabeth acknowledged that, because of her family history, she had been waiting for many years for the cancer to come to her, and there was a kind of relief that the waiting was over.

Dialogues with aspects of self, or subpersonalities (Rowan 1990), can help clients connect to the parts of themselves that may have been repressed, underdeveloped, or were simply unacknowledged. When these symbolic selves are given voices, they are often more readily integrated with the Whole Self—the healthier and more cohesive self.

Dialogues with older or younger selves give voice to experience. In the case of survivors of sexual abuse or domestic violence, these can often take the form of the *survivor self* talking with the *abused self*. Writing a dialogue with the *child self* can allow the child-who-once-was to tell her story and be listened to, perhaps for the first time.

The dialogue Carrie wrote with her child self was almost the first time she had connected with the events of her childhood, when she was abused by her father and unprotected by her mother.

Adult Carrie: *Hello, little child, I wonder if you can tell me what happened to you?*

Little Child: *I'm not allowed to tell you, nobody must know, he said it's our secret. I tried to tell mummy but . . .*

AC: *So mummy did know—I wasn't sure.*

LC: *I'm dirty, it's my fault, you don't want to listen.*

AC: *But I do, I do, I'm sorry I didn't listen before, I want to know.*

LC: *NONONONO, mustn't mustn't mustn't go away leave me alone not my friend can't tell you must stay awake must stay awake can't tell dirty dirty dirty don't tell anyone it didn't happen must be lying you don't care.*

AC: *Dear little child, please don't hide. I do believe you. I know you aren't a liar. It wasn't your fault. Kate believes you, too—she'll believe us and she says it isn't our fault. Let us love you.*

LC: *Can you really? Not sure I can trust you yet.*

AC: *But you can and I hope you will. Thank you for talking to me today. Do you think we can talk again?*

LC: *Perhaps, yes, maybe, I want to go now though.*

Feedback:

> *When I read this there are tears falling down my face again. The pain of the little girl who wouldn't be believed, who thought it must be her fault. It's almost unbearable. But I begin to think that it wasn't my fault, I know it wasn't really but I don't "feel" it yet.*

Perspectives

The *perspectives* journal technique (Adams, 1990, 2006) gives clients an opportunity to see things in a different way, whether by projecting forward or backward in time, following roads not taken, or changing the voice of the writer, such as switching from first-person narrator (I) to third person (he, she, it).

Changing the perspective of time by jumping forward into the future can help people see beyond current anxiety. Claire was a student in a counseling program preparing for her final presentation; she was in the grip of debilitating performance anxiety. She dated her page ahead to the day of her presentation and wrote:

> *In a few minutes that door will open and I'll be invited in to show my video to the panel. I've got the tape here, the notes for my commentary. I feel about 11 years old (performance anxiety, yucky). I wish the ground would swallow me up,*

there'd be an earthquake so I didn't have to do this and we'd all have something else to think about. But I know I'm ready. The tape is good, and I know it backwards (going through it over and over again really helped, even though I hated even putting it in the machine at first). I could stand on my head and do it! These people are not my enemies. I can do this!

Feedback:

I do feel much better about it having really thought about it, having pictured it. I also recognize it is important for me to really, really, really do the preparation and look at the tape so that it is true I know it backwards. I have been so petrified that I can't even bring myself to look at it on my own. I can now plan times to do this (Thompson 2011, 154).

It is also useful to change perspectives and write from another's point of view. Renee was still deeply grieving for her husband, but she wanted to start to live her own life again. She felt guilty about thinking about taking a vacation without him. Writing a perspectives entry from his perspective helped her to feel that he would encourage her plans to begin to live more independently.

Journal Writing as Self-Supervision

The same classic journal techniques, used for self-supervision or professional support, offer many benefits to counselors. These include:

- a different way of reflecting on the therapeutic relationship (including transference and countertransference)
- supporting the professional self through a form of observation and inner work
- seeing things about a client or session differently
- identifying and overcoming blind spots
- developing new perspectives
- clarifying thinking
- witnessing the practice and developing a unique practitioner narrative

Let us explore these benefits through three familiar techniques—captured moments, unsent letters, and dialogues—as expressed in the journals of counselors I supervise.

Captured Moments

Captured moments written at the end of a client session can bring into focus details of the session that might otherwise escape or evade conscious memory. This technique also offers an opportunity to revisit particular times and reflect more deeply on different elements of the interaction or setting.

You are my last client on Tuesday. The room is filled with the imprint of previous sessions, and I am ready to go home. Usually you come and we talk and you go and it's not clear that anything much happens. But now something does.

I watch you and listen to you as you pour out your sadness. We are enveloped in it. You are dressed in your normal, smart, pleated skirt and twinset but your face has lost its well-pressed, immaculately made-up appearance. It's a bit shocking, I'm seeing you naked. I'm momentarily distracted by thinking about where you can go to repair and recover your façade before returning to your world. I think I wanted to go, to escape—which of course I can. The sadness was so raw and so unexpected that for a moment it was unbearable. Your eyes hold me as if you want to be sure I stay there. I realize we have moved to another level of our work and relationship and your relationship with your pain. (Thompson 2011, 201)

Unsent Letters

This technique is particularly useful for identifying and working with transference and countertransference (that is, when thoughts and feelings from previous relationships or situations in the client's or counselor's life become revived in the counseling relationship). Speaking "the unspeakable" in an unsent letter helped a supervisee, Lily, understand crucial interactions and how her own previous experience was showing up in her session with a woman a generation older than her:

Dear J,
You sit there and I find I'm wondering how we really are doing. I wonder if I'm meeting your expectations and helping you. When you were talking about

your daughter and how her lifestyle was not one you could approve of, I found you were being quite disapproving—I felt your disapproval. I understand that, I really do. Your daughter hasn't fulfilled your hopes and expectations for her. She hasn't validated the struggle you went through as a single mum raising a child, something you never expected to have to do.

I have sensed your resistance from the start and wondered if maybe this counseling relationship wasn't going to be a big transformation for you since you were skeptical about getting started. But you come each week, we sit together, and I want to try harder. I want to lift your sense of disappointment and the feeling of being let down over and over again. I don't want to let you down.

Lily ended the letter there because she had a sudden flash of insight. She reflected:

Feedback:

When I read this I suddenly understand it's all that old mother-daughter stuff. I was suddenly again the daughter who wanted her mother's approval. Up it comes again! I know that J. is not my mother and I am the professional in this relationship.

By revealing, naming, and processing her countertransference in her journal, Lily was able to recalibrate her place in the counseling relationship and proceed with offering her client the therapeutic experience she wanted and needed.

Unsent letters to clients enable us to look at the relationship and the issues and reflect from outside the room. Here's an example of an unsent letter I wrote after a few sessions with a client where I was aware of a level of frustration, the source of which was not obvious:

Dear Anna,

I've been thinking about our session this afternoon. You seemed down again today. This felt different from the last time me met (which I know was a while ago—you cancelled our last meeting—you left a phone message for me earlier that day). I suppose a lot of time had elapsed—plenty of time for things to change or not to stay the same.

You were very angry again—angry with brother, angry with sister, and especially angry with mum. I felt a sinking feeling as the anger filled the room. Does your anger cover your own despair? There was no room for me.

I felt drained by the end of our session. Drained and a bit hopeless. Is that how you felt? How do you feel after our sessions—is this it—is this why you cancel some? Does it feel unsustainable? I wonder if I can say some of this to you—perhaps that would help. I remember your energy of the previous session—that was what felt different. I hope to see you next week.

All good wishes,

Kate

Feedback:

Writing this helped me to realize that I was feeling rejected (that "poor me" sense)—"there was no room for me" said a lot. (Thompson 2011, 202)

Dialogue with Practitioner Self

Sometimes the professional self can have different agenda from the private self. Writing a dialogue between the two identities is a way of exploring this. This technique can be helpful in making decisions and working through career changes or transitions as well as organizational issues. It is also something that can help us look at our life/work balance. Here's a dialogue between Self and Practitioner Self:

S: *Are you satisfied by your work at the moment?*

PS: *What do you think? I wonder why you are asking me this.*

S: *That's typical of you, isn't it? I ask you a question and you answer with a question—you deflect it away from yourself every time.*

PS: *It's my job. And you aren't being very helpful when you ask those questions—it's just distracting and I've got too much to do right now to start that kind of nebulous thinking.*

S: *That seems to be the problem—you do have too much to do, you're getting overwhelmed, and I can see that you aren't keeping up with things—look at that pile of letters to type, forms to fill, paper everywhere, and I bet some of it is overdue.*

PS: *Yes, well, it's alright for you, you leave me to deal with all this and then you expect me to come home ready to relax and socialize and do culture. Be bright and shiny with your friends. Don't you get it? I DO NOT HAVE TIME.*

S: *You are really feeling exhausted, aren't you? What can I do to help?*

PS: *Thank you for asking (at last). But if you really want to help you could begin by not accepting every invitation, not agreeing to every social arrangement, and maybe, perhaps, you could spend a bit of time with me, we could maybe look at all these piles of paper. Sometimes I'm not sure where to begin.*

S: *Of course I can, we'll do it together, it's not so bad really—and if we don't go out this weekend we'll probably get it sorted.*

PS: *Oh, thank you—I really need your organizing/decluttering skills—I know you have those—the rest of the house is immaculate—it's only my office.*

S: *You're welcome—it'll be a pleasure—it won't be a problem now.*

Feedback: *When I look at this the phrase "burning the candle at both ends" springs to mind. I am normally very organized and tidy, but somehow I'd let the paperwork for my practice build up, and I'd become rather scared of tackling it. Now I know what I need to do next.*

Conclusion

Once clients and counselors begin using journal writing as part of the counseling process, they frequently say, "I didn't know there were so many different ways to write a journal, or that it would be as helpful as it is." They express surprise at the range of techniques that can be used and the depth of insight that can be gained in a relatively short time. The combination of technique, expression, and feedback (reflection) seems to be what makes journal writing a powerful therapeutic technique and brings access to deeper levels of self-support and healing.

References

Adams, Kathleen. 1990. *Journal to the self: Twenty-two paths to personal growth.* New York: Grand Central Publishing (originally Warner Books).

———. 1999. Writing as therapy. *Counseling and Human Development* 31 (5): January 1999.

———. 2006. *Journal therapy: Writing as a therapeutic tool: A training workbook.* Brentwood, TN: Cross Country Education.

Michaels, Anne. 2000. The hooded hawk. In *Poems.* London: Bloomsbury.

Progoff, Ira. 1992. *At a journal workshop.* Los Angeles: Jeremy P. Tarcher Publishers.

Rowan, John. 1990. *Subpersonalities: The people inside us.* London: Routledge.

Thompson, Kate. 2004. Journal writing as a therapeutic tool. In *Writing cures: An introductory handbook of writing in counselling and therapy.* Gillie Bolton, et al., eds. London: Routledge.

———. 2011. *Therapeutic journal writing.* London: Jessica Kingsley Publishers.

Note

1. In the National Health System, mental health is integrated with medical health care.

Liberating Beauty: The Hynes and Hynes-Berry Bibliotherapy Model

JOY ROULIER SAWYER

The growing field of expressive writing fosters many vibrant branches of professional training and practice. One notable theoretical contribution to the development of expressive writing standards can be found in the branch known as *bibliotherapy*.

Biblio/Poetry Therapy—The Interactive Process: A Handbook by Arleen McCarty Hynes and Mary Hynes-Berry (1994, 2012) is an essential text for professional training through the National Federation for Biblio/Poetry Therapy (NFBPT),[1] the credentialing board for poetry therapists and other expressive writing specialists. The authors define *bibliotherapy* in this manner: "Bibliotherapy uses literature to bring about a therapeutic interaction between participant and facilitator" (2012, 3). Throughout the textbook, they use the terms *interactive bibliotherapy*, *biblio/poetry therapy*, and *poetry therapy* synonymously (5). Many practitioners consider the Hynes and Hynes-Berry text to be the "bible" of poetry therapy training, as one of the authors, Arleen McCarty Hynes, was instrumental in creating best-practice standards for the field (Heller 2012, xvii–xix).

To attain credentials in biblio/poetry therapy, students complete a rigorous training program that includes theory and practicum in poetry therapy, journal therapy, creative writing, and group facilitation. Required readings and class work include basics of psychology and standards of ethical practice. Students with educational backgrounds and degrees in developmental (nonclinical) fields such as education and creative writing are certified as applied poetry facilitators (CAPF). Those with educational backgrounds andlicensure as mental health counselors, psychotherapists, social workers, psychologists, and psychiatrists are credentialed as certified (CPT) or registered (PTR) poetry therapists (NFBPT 2012, 13). Expressive writing plays a major role in the facilitative work of many NFBPT credential holders. In an online survey of experienced, credentialed practitioners, the majority reported that they always, or almost always, include an expressive writing component in their poetry therapy facilitations (Adams and Sawyer 2012).

Unique Aspects of the Hynes and Hynes-Berry Model in Expressive Writing

The Hynes and Hynes-Berry four-stage bibliotherapy model makes a unique contribution to the field of expressive writing in that it uses literature as a catalyst for the writing process: "[t]he bibliotherapeutic process depends at least in part on the way the participants relate to a stimulus that has its own *language-based coherence and integrity*" (Hynes and Hynes-Berry 2012, 6, italics in the original). Although poems are most often used in interactive bibliotherapeutic sessions, Hynes and Hynes-Berry's literature categories include films, music lyrics, short stories, novels, essays, magazine articles—almost anything solely language-based (6).

The Hynes and Hynes-Berry bibliotherapeutic model in expressive writing practice differs from other models in that it relies upon something *outside the self* to evoke a personal response, which eventually leads to the writing process. Rather than relying primarily on self-generated writing, such as journal therapy does, the model is dependent upon the client's or participant's engagement with a carefully selected text to help nourish self-expression: "*Bibliotherapy stimulates the mind and imagination, allows an experience of the liberating quality of beauty, provides focus, and facilitates the recognition and understanding of feelings*" (16, italics in the original).

One unique aspect of the model's therapeutic goals provides the foundation for the facilitator's approach in choosing literature: "*Where beauty is perceived, an integration of self takes place*" (17–18, italics in the original). The authors believe that by responding to the liberating beauty of a well-crafted piece of literature, the participant experiences momentary pleasure—a pleasure that encourages renewed appreciation and awareness of the outside world, thus encouraging the freedom to simply *be*, free from the demands of the self (17–18). As many practicing poetry therapists can attest, the healing power of beauty—particularly the literary beauty found in poetry, fiction, plays, film, or music lyrics—is powerful indeed, ripe with remarkable potential for therapeutic insight, awareness, compassion, and change. Hynes and Hynes-Berry build their bibliotherapy model on this very simple, yet profound, concept.

Although the authors note that an "experience of beauty" may not occur in every bibliotherapy session, it is this liberating aspect of spontaneous pleasure and delight that remains at the heart and soul of the theory. The fresh perspective offered by meaningful literature stimulates the imagination, which provides a nurturing context for the participant's own personal expressive writing to eventually take place. Thus, it is the participant's *feeling-response* to beauty (or personal meaning) that helps facilitate the four main goals of bibliotherapy:

1. to improve the capacity to respond by stimulating and enriching mental images and concepts and by helping the feelings about these images to surface
2. to increase self-understanding by helping individuals value their own personhood and become more knowledgeable and more accurate about self-perceptions
3. to increase awareness of interpersonal relationships
4. to improve reality orientation (15)

A Brief Introduction to the Hynes and Hynes-Berry Biblio/Poetry Therapy Model

The essential core of the model is found in chapter 3, "The Bibliotherapeutic Process," which describes the four-step process, and chapter 4, "Criteria for Choosing Bibliotherapeutic Materials," which provides eight essential criteria for selecting poetry and other literature for bibliotherapeutic use (31–67). In addition to its use as a stand-alone therapeutic process, practicing professional clinicians can also integrate the interactive bibliotherapy model into other therapeutic modalities; it is not directly tied to any specific school of thought—psychoanalytic, psychodynamic, cognitive-behavioral, or other (33). For those working in developmental (nonclinical) settings such as schools, churches, and synagogues, the model is easily adaptable as well.

The four major process steps of biblio/poetry therapy are *recognition, examination, juxtaposition, and application to self* (31). Although these four process steps are often described as "stages," the model in practice often involves an overlapping and fluid interplay among the four elements (42). In other words, it is not necessary that participants experience these four stages sequentially, but the model often gently unfolds in the following manner.

Recognition

The recognition step is found in the initial response to the poetry or literature. "There is something in the material that *engages* the participant—something that piques interest, opens the imagination, stops wandering thoughts, or in some way arrests attention" (33). This is the previously mentioned personal response to beauty, meaning, or intrigue that uniquely initiates the expressive writing process. One of the most refreshing aspects of the model is that this stage encourages participants to *respond emotionally or viscerally* to a poem, rather than offer literary analysis or critique. So during this phase of the model, questions like "Does anything in this poem speak to you? Any lines or images or rhythms you especially like or enjoy?" provide an open-ended context that allows the participants to offer their initial, spontaneous responses.

Examination

Recognition is followed by *examination*—an intensified version of the first step that involves deepened questioning and responses to the literature (37). As the participants voice their variety of responses, this is the stage where the facilitator often follows with questions designed to encourage even more personal reflection: "You mentioned earlier that this poem reminds you of summers you spent on your grandmother's farm. Can you say more?" Over time, as the group begins to congeal, the participants often begin to initiate asking some of these "curious" questions of each other. There is always more below the surface of an initial response to the poem, and the variety of experiences voiced provides a context for deepened exploration of beauty or personal meaning.

Juxtaposition

The third step, *juxtaposition*, involves "the act of putting side by side, for purposes of comparison and contrast, two impressions of an object or experience" (38). The participant weighs his or her original response to the literature next to the varieties of responses from the group, which can result in an even deeper confirmation of the original response, changes in perspective due to the input of others, or perhaps the recognition of the need for even more time and space to process personal feelings (39).

This is usually one of the most communally gratifying aspects of the model, as participants often learn and grow from one another's responses, as well as discover new insights into their own, original feelings and responses to the poem. Sometimes, participants even experience a completely different shift in perspective—one of the results of relating to others in a neutral meeting ground of beauty and meaning.

Application to Self

The final step, *application to self*, is the process of integrating the new insights into real-life experience to "make a personal commitment to using the new attitudes as a reference point for response or action" (40–41). As participants begin to reflect on their personal experiences with the poem, they are encouraged to find ways to integrate their learning and understanding into daily life. Emotional responses, memories, new ideas, alternative ways of thinking—all of these are material for the participants to choose new ways of practical action and living in the world.

Choosing Literature for Bibliotherapy

The criteria for literature selection in a Hynes and Hynes-Berry bibliotherapy session differs from criteria often applied in academic literature courses. Poems, short stories, films, and other forms of language-based prompts are chosen for particular therapeutic qualities, which include: universal experience of emotion (particular to the individual/group); powerful; comprehensible; positive; compelling rhythm; imagery (striking, concrete); language (simple, precise vocabulary; clear, simple diction); and complexity (manageable length, succinct) (52–53).

It is important to note that, by offering the "positive" criteria for literature selection, Hynes and Hynes-Berry are not advocating for excluding emotionally difficult material: "Rather, good bibliotherapeutic material will help identify negative feelings in a way that will lead to liberating action" (57). The authors echo the theoretical thinking of another poetry therapy pioneer, Dr. Jack J. Leedy (1985), who believed that the isoprinciple used in the selection of music for music therapy was also applicable to poetry therapy: "[p]oems that are close in feeling to the mood of the [participant] have been found helpful" (82). By reading poems that express difficult feelings, poetry therapy participants often begin to feel that they are not alone and that their feelings can be understood.

However, it is important to note that Leedy advises that poems that offer no hope, increase guilt feelings, fuel homicidal rage, or that mention suicide should not be used in poetry therapy (83). In other words, the sense of emotional identification the participant feels from the literature should result in empathy for themselves and others and thus to greater empowerment—which eventually can lead to positive forward movement.

Also, by using the term *simple* as it relates to language in literature selection criteria, the authors do not mean *simplistic*. Instead, they recommend choosing literature that does not sacrifice a feeling response because it requires too much intellectual grappling or difficulty in reading or pronunciation by the participant (Hynes and Hynes-Berry 2012, 61).

An Educational Adaptation in a Developmental Expressive Writing Setting: A Contextual Approach

For nearly a decade, I have cotaught with Kathleen Adams a course called "Writing and Healing" in the Masters of Liberal Studies department at University College, University of Denver.[2] The current course is uniquely structured in that it is not taught within a graduate psychology or counseling program but instead as part of a creative writing track in the Arts and Culture division. It often attracts elementary, middle school, and high school educators, as well as creative writers looking to deepen and enrich their literary work and creative process.

We take several elements into account when structuring our classroom experiences for educators and writers, and these elements differ from training and educational opportunities we have provided for professional therapists and facilitators. For one, therapists/facilitators introduced to the Hynes and Hynes-Berry model do not have the application limitations that educators do—limitations such as course objectives, curriculum planning, grading requirements, and other circumstances. A clearly defined bibliotherapy group differs from a standard literature class in both its approach to, and goals for, the use of the literature.

In the literature classroom, the object of the discussion is usually literary analysis, with emphasis on historical context, identifying literary themes, various craft elements, and other literary applications. The teacher is largely responsible for providing the insights gleaned from the literature, as well as correct interpretations of the text (Hynes and Hynes-Berry 2012, 32). The purpose of literature in a bibliotherapeutic context, however, is quite different:

In bibliotherapy . . . the value of the literature depends strictly on its capacity to encourage a therapeutic (feeling) response from the participants. The individual's feeling-response is more important than an intellectual grasp of the work's meaning. Thus, in bibliotherapy *even a misinterpretation of the text is considered both legitimate and useful if it leads to the release of feelings or insights related to self-understanding.* In other words, the use of literature in bibliotherapy reflects the *goals of therapy* rather than *those of education.* (32, italics in the original)

The bibliotherapy facilitator's role is not to ensure that the text is correctly interpreted or understood; it is to facilitate emotional, personal responses to the literature. If we were to diagram the difference, it would look like figure 5.1 (the standard classroom model) and figure 5.2 (the bibliotherapy model).

In the standard literature classroom, the teacher is the primary facilitator, offering insight and analysis into the text. In a bibliotherapy group, however, the *literature itself actually becomes the primary facilitator.* The bibliotherapy facilitator's role is to keep gently returning the group's focus to the text and to encourage the sharing of personal responses (32).

Since the primary goal of bibliotherapy is a *feeling* response that leads to self-understanding, it is often not possible to strictly follow this approach in a traditional literature or creative writing classroom. For this reason, Adams and I encourage educators to adapt and integrate helpful aspects of the Hynes and Hynes-Berry model as they are able—aspects that bridge both good, solid literary criteria and the facilitation of more personally enriching, enlightening classroom discussions.

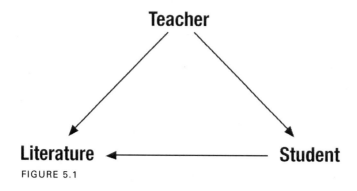

FIGURE 5.1

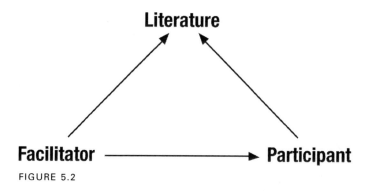

Literature

Facilitator ⟶ Participant

FIGURE 5.2

Over the years, many educators who have taken our class say that they find that the chapter 4 bibliotherapeutic literature criteria also closely parallel general rules of good literature selection. They also say that portions of the bibliotherapeutic model are easily adaptable for their own educational goals and purposes. In addition, several educators at various levels—elementary, high school, college—have enthusiastically reported successfully integrating portions of the model into their classroom discussions, particularly for creative writing coursework. In fact, I have used this educational approach in coteaching two other University College creative writing classes with another poetry therapy colleague. Since both of us hold creative writing–related graduate degrees, we chose a classroom approach that combined the Hynes and Hynes-Berry model of literature selection with a focus on certain writing craft elements.

This highlights another important feature of the Hynes and Hynes-Berry model: Because it is both creative and flexible, it can be easily adapted for a variety of contexts. In addition to its use by therapists and educators, it has also been used in religious, pastoral, and/or spiritual direction settings (Hynes and Hynes-Berry 2012). Within a Christian spiritual context, I have adapted the Hynes and Hynes-Berry model for individual clinical pastoral psychotherapeutic work in which the client's own poetry serves as the facilitating literature for future writing directions, using the four steps as passage markers in the client's spiritual and psychological growth (Sawyer 2004).

I have also expanded the model into a developmental metaphor for community nurture, exploring the idea of "communities as poems"—collective works of human art to be read, savored, and enjoyed, with the "self-application" stage resulting in thoughtful, reflective daily action for the sake of one's community (Sawyer 2005). It is my hope that a new generation of poetry therapy practitioners will continue to further explore and widen the application boundaries of the model into even more diverse and creative therapeutic and developmental venues.

Writing and Healing Classroom Structure and Content

Because our Writing and Healing course objectives include personal growth and self-understanding, the Hynes and Hynes-Berry model in our classroom facilitation is applied much as it would be with a bibliotherapy or poetry therapy group. Poetry is chosen that addresses personal growth and developmental (nonclinical) life span issues: birth, death, relationships, life transitions—in other words, experiences and challenges that are universal to the human condition. Students are guided through an experience of what it is actually like to be in a bibliotherapy group, with the added educational benefit of "stepping back" from the process at the end to explore and discuss how the group progressed through the four stages of the Hynes and Hynes-Berry model.

Each three-hour classroom experience is designed in two parts. The first half focuses on discussions of theoretical readings, during which students respond to and apply their learning from a variety of therapeutic writing theorists and theoretical structures introduced into the coursework (Adams 1990, 1999; Progoff 1992; Pennebaker 2004; Jacobs 2004; DeSalvo 1999; Rosen 2010; Hynes and Hynes-Berry 1994, 2012). Louise DeSalvo's *Writing as a Way of Healing: How Telling Stories Transforms Our Lives* (1999) is particularly helpful for the creative writing context in which we teach. DeSalvo, an English professor at Hunter College (and a nontherapist), addresses the subject of writing and healing from a literary perspective. Another useful text is performance poet Kim Rosen's *Saved by a Poem: The Transformative Power of Words* (2010), which explores several meaningful poems that correspond closely to Hynes and Hynes-Berry literature selection criteria and are often used in poetry therapy venues. The book includes a CD of readings of each of the poems, accompanied by music.

The second half of the class is facilitated much like a poetry therapy group experience. We open with an expressive writing warm-up exercise that usually foreshadows the theme of the selected poem. After sharing and discussion of the warm-up write, the poem is presented to read aloud together, sometimes followed by an audio reading from Rosen's CD, if the poem is represented there. Together, the students "sit" with the poem, savoring it, calling out favorite lines or phrases, images that resonate or move them, and appealing rhythms or thoughts. There is a guided conversation about how the poem speaks, or doesn't, to current life situations. The class sifts and sorts and questions and ponders, unearthing nuggets of personal feeling, insight, and memory. Class members voice disparate ways the poem affects them, a potpourri of ideas and thoughts. As teachers and group facilitators, we are careful not to impose a "right" or "best" way to read the poem. We encourage each person's unique contribution as they contrast/compare (juxtapose) their own personal responses to those of their classmates'.

As our poetry conversation draws to a close, the class is given an expressive writing prompt that is specifically designed to help facilitate application to self, the fourth step in the Hynes and Hynes-Berry process. This can take the form of a journal write, a poem, a stream-of-consciousness write—virtually anything written, prompted by the catalytic poem. Students are then encouraged to follow their expressive writes with what we call a *reflection write* (see Adams, chapter 1). We ask our students to reread what they have just written, and then to write a sentence or two in response to their writing, paying special attention to what they noticed in themselves as they wrote. We also encourage students to circle or underline particularly resonant passages that they'd like to return to, for either future journal or poetry writing.

As we finish the writing process, we will often open the second discussion portion with the question, "What was this writing exercise like for you?" Most students then share their varied experiences and feelings about the writing process, rather than the write itself. There is also room for those who are eager to read their expressive writes out loud. We then "step back" from the process and return to teaching mode in order to deconstruct the Hynes and

Hynes-Berry model and discuss how the group recognized and experienced it during our facilitated session.

Observations on Classroom Effects of the Hynes and Hynes-Berry Model

Since 2003, Adams and I have cotaught the DU Writing and Healing class about fifteen times, both in the classroom and online. Because there is a wide age range (twenty-five to sixty-five) among our students, as well as great diversity in terms of vocation, life experience, and religious and political beliefs, the Hynes and Hynes-Berry universality criteria prove especially helpful for our classroom literature selections. We have used a diverse selection of poems over the years, and over time some favorite, dependable bibliotherapy selections have emerged. Poems such as Mary Oliver's "The Summer Day" (1992) or Li-Young Lee's "From Blossoms" (1986) or Tony Hoagland's "The Word" (1992) embrace a broad population in personal appeal and popularity.

What is truly remarkable is to watch how, over the course of ten weeks, poetry and expressive writing enhance the level of understanding, compassion, and creative growth that develops among our students. Genuinely life- and perspective-changing conversations often emerge between students who might not otherwise connect over the water cooler at work, or who might stand on opposite sides of a political picket line.

By gently guiding the conversation around individual reflections about poems (not "right" or "wrong" responses, or critical literary analyses) as well as protecting our students' privacy by assuring them that their expressive writing does not necessarily need to be shared with others, we have observed that the gateway opens for deeper emotional responses, creative experimentation, and greater freedom of expressive writing.

The model fosters a nonhierarchical, collaborative culture within the classroom. Since the poem acts as the main "facilitator," as the session progresses the participants begin to look more and more to the literature, and to each other, as opposed to us as teachers/facilitators. This experience usually enhances the expressive writing process. The poem itself serves as a creative catalyst for the students, and we will often use one poetry line as a writing prompt, or ask participants to choose a particularly enjoyable or meaningful poetry line with which to begin. They also have the benefit of hearing the collective wisdom and experiences of their classmates, which augments their own writing process.

Particularly helpful to the expressive writing process is the result of what occurs in the "juxtaposition" step of the Hynes and Hynes-Berry model. It is then that the shared responses and feelings of classmates either provide a different lens for a participant or may confirm more deeply their original response to the poem. This collective input can often be observed when class members share either their responses to the writing exercise or the write itself. The shared sense that a group feels from both discussing a poem and then participating together in a poetry or expressive writing exercise is markedly different from that of a journal writing session. The shared focus of something outside the self provides a neutral ground in which all different kinds of people from various walks of life can meet and learn from a common human experience via a poem, especially chosen for its beauty, meaningfulness, emotional relevance, or any other number of personal growth reasons. Conversations also often broaden to include larger global or social themes as they relate to the students' personal feelings and experiences.

Integrating a Hynes and Hynes-Berry Approach into Expressive Writing Assignments

Classroom homework assignments also reflect portions of the Hynes and Hynes-Berry model, in which the actual expressive write (journaling or poetry) is not graded or even seen by us, unless the student wishes to include it. Rather, we ask for a one- to two-page reflection write on the expressive writing exercise itself, which we explain to our students in the following manner:

A reflection piece is pondering the writing process you just engaged in. For example, what did you become aware of as you wrote? What was going on in your body? What writing ideas came to mind as you wrote this particular piece? Were you surprised by anything? Disappointed? Delighted? You are free to write about anything and everything you might feel or notice, as long as it focuses on the **writing process itself**. This way of writing requires of you that you maintain simultaneous perspective. On one level, you are engaged in the actual writing of your own journal entry/poem/story, etc. On another level, you are observing yourself as you wrote with a sort of detached curiosity. (Adams and Sawyer 2007)

Students are asked to participate in a two-part process: 1) to engage in an initial expressive write (journaling or poetry) in response to an assigned poem and prompt, and 2) to write a reflection piece, based on his or her observations of the expressive writing process. We also note that, although the students are welcome to include their original creative write, we will only respond to the reflection write. This enables us to give the student feedback on his or her engagement with the writing process while allowing the expressive write to remain both personal and ungraded.

Here is an example of how a Hynes and Hynes-Berry model is used in an expressive writing assignment: We ask students to read (and to listen on Rosen's CD, if they wish) a poem by Naomi Shihab Nye, "Kindness" (1995), which beautifully exemplifies the Hynes and Hynes-Berry literature selection criteria categories (Rosen 2010, 78–79). Nye's poem is a thoughtful, touching, well-crafted work on a variety of ways in which kindness is a deep and essential part of our human experience. Students are then invited to write a poem or journal entry in response to the poem, paying careful attention to how the poem moves them, or how it might speak to their own personal experiences of kindness. As a writing prompt, we might ask, "What does kindness look like to you? You may want to personify kindness, or write about a time when you were grateful to receive the kindness of a family member, friend, colleague, or stranger" (Adams and Sawyer 2010).

After the students finish their expressive writes, they are invited to "step back" and write a one- to two-page reflection. This reflection writing process continues the deepening of engagement with the poem, and it builds upon the students' skills for learning (and moving forward) from their own expression. Sometimes students spontaneously refer back to specific Hynes and Hynes-Berry stages (reflection, examination, juxtaposition, and application to self) that they have observed in their own expressive writing experience. The student can return to the Hynes and Hynes-Berry model as a "structured container" in reflecting on other personal expressive writes, much the way the student can use yet another structured container we teach in our writing and healing coursework, the Journal Ladder (Adams 1999; see Adams, chapter 3).

Finally, yet another important dimension of our Hynes and Hynes-Berry bibliotherapy work in the classroom includes the privilege of introducing students to the rich contributions of our field's own poet-practitioners. A poem by poetry therapist Perie Longo (1997), "The Writing Circle," closes

The Writing Circle
with joy we sit we cry
we confess we are sorry
we are anxious we are tongue-
tied we are heart bound we are
safe we are falling off the cliff of
our hearts into a pool of clear water
so blue we think we are whales we breach
cry breathe burst forth like bulls through the gate
headfirst into the cape of our lives china splinters
translucent under an eclipsed moon oh watch us
jump over mercy leap with our capes like wings
that leave us splendid as never before we hover
on a scarf of air wafted in from somewhere
we have never been but plan to go as soon
as possible yes we are speaking untying
our tongues no longer sorry and then
we come down and return to where
we came from but something
is different we are smiling
our minds blue and falling
and nothing hurts amen.
—Perie Longo

many classroom experiences, as well as serving as a writing prompt for the final homework assignment.

This poem, which also demonstrates many strong aspects of the Hynes and Hynes-Berry literature criteria, provides a gentle launching pad from which our students can explore, discuss, and write about their various experiences of our writing and healing group work, as well as offer an avenue of reflective closure for their classroom experience.

Academic rigor need not be compromised in an expressive writing context. The final classroom assignment is a ten-page, personal application research paper on a writing and healing topic of interest. Students have presented outstanding final papers on diverse topics such as using writing and healing in divorce recovery, working with at-risk youth, using poetry as a learning intervention with autism spectrum disorder, navigating career transitions, developing a journal program for weight management, coping with grief and loss, creating a bibliotherapeutic approach for the youngest readers (K–3) using picture books with emotionally intelligent themes, and many others.

Conclusion

This demonstration is but one example of how the Hynes and Hynes-Berry model can be integrated into a liberal arts masters-level curriculum. The structure of the University of Denver Writing and Healing coursework could easily be adapted for college-level psychology and counseling classes, or even creative writing classes, as a basic introduction course to therapeutic or expressive writing.

The positive effects of Hynes and Hynes-Berry's bibliotherapy theory, firmly grounded in beauty's therapeutic potential, have been reflected in the classroom many times over. As the authors state, there is indeed transformative power to be found in a personal encounter with a vibrant, life-giving poem. Classroom activities such as a guided discussion of meaningful literature, a personally expressive write, and a reflection write offer students spiritual respite and a welcome balm in the midst of an often frenetic, media-saturated culture.

As the expressive writing field continues to expand and develop, the Hynes and Hynes-Berry bibliotherapy model remains a unique—and important—

theoretical contribution, a foundational framework that can provide robust support for the future growth and vitality of expressive writing coursework within university and college settings. The liberating power of beauty is indeed alive and well.

References

Adams, Kathleen. 1990. *Journal to the self: Twenty-two paths to personal growth.* New York: Warner Books.

———. 1999. Writing as therapy. *Counseling and Human Development* 31: 1–16.

Adams, Kathleen, and Joy R. Sawyer. 2007. How to write a reflection piece. Writing and Healing course, University College, University of Denver.

———. 2010. Example of weekly expressive writing assignment. Writing and Healing course, University College, University of Denver.

———. 2012. NFBPT-credentialed mentor/supervisor research survey, June 2012. Online survey. Center for Journal Therapy, Denver, CO. http://survey. constantcontact. com/surveya07e60ggktxh36evth1/results (accessed June 19, 2012).

DeSalvo, Louise. 1999. *Writing as a way of healing: How telling our stories transforms our lives.* San Francisco: HarperSanFrancisco.

Heller, Peggy Osna. 2012. Introduction to third edition. In *Biblio/Poetry Therapy— The Interactive Process: A Handbook*, 3rd ed. Arleen McCarty Hynes and Mary Hynes Berry. St. Cloud, MN: North Star Press of St. Cloud, Inc.

Hoagland, Tony. 1992. The word. In *Sweet ruin*. Madison, WI: University of Wisconsin Press.

Hynes, Arleen McCarty, and Mary Hynes-Berry. 2012. *Biblio/Poetry Therapy—The Interactive Process: A Handbook*, 3rd ed. St. Cloud, MN: North Star Press of St. Cloud, Inc. (orig. pub. 1994).

Jacobs, Beth. 2004. *Writing for emotional balance: A guided journal to help you manage overwhelming emotions*. Oakland, CA: New Harbinger Publications, Inc.

Lee, Li-Young. 1986. From blossoms. In *From blossoms: Selected poems*. Northumberland, UK: Bloodaxe.

Leedy, Jack J. 1985. Principles of poetry therapy. In *Poetry as healer: Mending the troubled mind.* Jack J. Leedy, ed. New York: Vanguard Press.

Longo, Perie. 1997. The writing circle. Originally published as The writing group in *The privacy of wind: Poems by Perie Longo.* Santa Barbara, CA: John Daniel and Co. This version is used at request and by permission of the poet.

National Federation for Biblio/Poetry Therapy. 2012. *Guide to training requirements for certification and registration in poetry therapy.* Steamboat Springs, CO: NFBPT.

Nye, Naomi Shihab. 1995. Kindness. In *Saved by a poem: The transformative power of words.* Kim Rosen. Carlsbad, CA: Hay House, 2010.

Oliver, Mary. 1992. The summer day. In *House of light.* Boston: Beacon Press.

Pennebaker, James W. 2004. *Writing to heal: A guided journal for recovering from trauma and emotional upheaval.* Oakland, CA: New Harbinger Publications.

Progoff, Ira. 1992. *At a journal workshop: Writing to access the power of the unconscious and evoke creative ability.* Los Angeles: Jeremy P. Tarcher, Inc.

Rosen, Kim. 2010. *Saved by a poem: The transformative power of words.* Carlsbad, CA: Hay House.

Sawyer, Joy R. 2004. Toward a pastoral psychotherapeutic context for poetry therapy: A poetry therapy process adaptation of the Hynes and Hynes-Berry biblio/poetry therapy model. *Journal of Poetry Therapy* 17: 155–63.

Sawyer, Joy R. 2005. The cry of the soul: Poetry therapy and beyond. Presentation. Transformative Language Arts Conference, Goddard College, Plainfield, VT.

Acknowledgments

The author gratefully acknowledges Mary Hynes-Berry and North Star Press of St. Cloud, Inc., who generously gave permission to reproduce material from *Biblio/Poetry Therapy—The Interactive Process: A Handbook* by Arleen McCarty Hynes and Mary Hynes-Berry (2012).

Grateful acknowledgment is also given to Perie Longo for permission to use her poem, "The Writing Circle." Other versions of this poem also appear in *Finding What You Didn't Lose* by John Fox (1995, Jeremy P. Tarcher) and *The Privacy of Wind: Poems by Perie Longo* (1997, John Daniel and Co.).

Notes

1. For more information on professional training, see NFBPT's website, www.nfbpt. com.

2. Our teaching work is made more professionally meaningful because Arleen Hynes taught some of her first bibliotherapy coursework at the University of Denver (Heller 2012, xviii).

6

Engaging the Reluctant Writer

LINDA BARNES

Natalie stares into space. The writing assignment she's just been given seems to have made no impression on her at all. From the outside, she appears carved in stone, inert, barely breathing. Inside, however, her mind is exploding into fireworks. Her thoughts shoot in every direction at once, flashing so brightly she can't focus on any single idea.

Meanwhile, Blake is scribbling furiously. After two or three sentences, he begins to cross words out vigorously, then immediately begins again. He fills most of the page this way, writing and striking out over and over until he gives an audible sigh and scrunches the paper into a wad for the wastebasket.

These writers are typical of the hundreds of students I've worked with in my years as a college counselor and instructor. I've had the privilege of working with community college students in support groups and for-credit writing classes as they adjust to the challenges and changes in their lives.

Again and again I have had the opportunity to coax students like Natalie and Blake into a new relationship with the writing process. I've celebrated with them the discovery that writing is powerful, and that their journals and poems can take them on unexpected journeys. My passion is encouraging the use of personal writing—journals and poems—to balance the demand for academic writing and critical thinking otherwise emphasized in higher education.

It has been my great fortune to work in an environment where both the dean of students and the chair of the Humanities Department endorsed the opportunity for our community college students to take elective classes in nonacademic, expressive writing, where the emphasis was on clear and thoughtful self-expression rather than the correct use of grammatical conventions and academic language.

Although students in my courses were typically coenrolled in academic composition classes, even in an environment of relaxed performance expectations they still struggled to write fluently and clearly. One of the requirements for passing composition classes is the necessity of writing a clear essay in one class sitting, a requirement many of our students struggled painfully to pass. Standard composition classes no longer have room for focus on expressive writing due to the demand to produce good academic writers. As a faculty member in the college counseling department, I was in a unique position to offer these courses and embraced the opportunity to challenge students to improve their writing fluency and speedy self-disclosure.

Mistaken beliefs about what makes a good writer or a good piece of writing often keep students from even beginning. If they do begin, more beliefs flood in that cause them to abandon initial ideas without time to incubate and grow. Students say they "can't think of anything to write about," or they've "never been a very good writer." Some believe they "work best under pressure," "can't write on demand," or "have nothing interesting to say."

When they are encouraged to challenge these beliefs with expressive writing, the students begin to change their thinking through having different experiences with their beliefs. They start to realize that these beliefs are phantoms, with little basis in actual reality. They then come into the embodied awareness that what they believe either helps or hinders them. They grasp that the process of writing is a metaphoric brain surgery, "operating" on their minds with words and experiences, transforming their negative beliefs into positive ones, and empowering them to move forward in writing and life.

In the process of changing their beliefs, the students learn that developing the capacity to write clearly about their experiences and reactions gives them a powerful tool for confronting challenges and meeting goals. Their pens become magic wands that dissolve obstacles and pave paths to more satisfactory futures. Even formal writing improves when students are encouraged to participate in the process of expressive writing.

The following are eight inhibiting beliefs my students have expressed about writing and writers, together with examples of how they have broken through these barriers to achieve greater self-confidence, more fluent writing, livelier work, and clearer thinking.

1. Only Certain Special People Can Be Called Writers

Recently I asked some of my students to define "a writer," and nearly all produced a definition that included having had something published. In fact, to most people, a writer is one whose scribblings have been externally validated, whose attempt at communicating via the written word has resulted in some outside authority—often a publisher—branding them as approved to have a public audience.

But what does it really mean to be a writer, or to be good at writing?

Humans seem to be born with an innate drive and desire for self-expression. Some have natural aptitude or interest in music, sports, art, dance, writing, performance, or other expressions. Parents and teachers often support children who demonstrate ability and interest in a particular area. But even in the absence of early aptitude or interest, the *basic skills* in all of these areas can be acquired. With intent and practice, most people can become reasonably good at several differing skills.

We all know how to sing, to dance, to laugh, and to fool around with paint, rhythm, motion, sound, and rhyme. A major part of debunking the mistaken belief that only certain people can be called writers is to reacquaint the students with their earlier enjoyment in playing with words.

I tell my students about my oldest son, Nigel, an accomplished artist. Nigel began drawing at the age of two, using crayons on the canvas of his bedroom wall. By the time he was in high school, his class notes consisted of iconographic drawings with brief written dates or special vocabulary words beside them. He once repeated an entire hour-long ancient history class lesson to me from four drawings and two written dates.

One day when I was admiring his drawing talent, he told me, "You could be an artist, too, Mom." I was shocked. "Me??" I asked. He replied, "Sure. Just draw something every day."

The same can be said about writing. Good writers are simply those that practice writing. A lot!

Having students make lists is one of the simplest and most effective ways to loosen up their writing selves. I like to begin by having them create a list called Things I Love, allowing just two or three minutes for the exercise. When time is up, students are invited to share their lists, one item at a time, around the room.

There is little hesitation with the sharing round. The students are eager to participate, as sharing what they enjoy is relatively low risk. I instruct them to share without comment or explanation, to be unconcerned with repetition since universal experiences often show up, and to borrow liberally from each other by writing down on their own lists anything they hear and resonate with.

As teachers, we can use these lists as an evaluation of the stage at which students have come to us. Hesitant, uncertain writers are sometimes stuck in the broad, concrete world of generalities. They may produce a list like this one:

List of Things I Love
ocean
pizza
my kids
chocolate
laughter
sunshine
blue

Compare this general list to that of someone who has developed her voice, fluency, and specificity to a greater degree:

Things I Love
the beach at Carmel, California
pepperoni pizza with lots of gooey cheese
Cadbury milk chocolate with hazelnuts
listening to my children laughing in the next room
sunlight filtered through redwood trees
a cobalt blue bottle on a sunny windowsill

Writers initially given to generalities can be nudged toward more vivid writing through the introduction of lists of lively and specific words (see exercise samples following this chapter), writing exercises appealing to the senses, and instructions to be as idiosyncratic, individual, and personal as they dare. I still remember a girl in one group who included *soda crackers with peanut butter and sardines* on her list.

The Things I Love list provides both an appeal to universality and a glimpse into the quirkiness that makes each of us unique. It actively demonstrates to students that all of us are "just like you, only different." It normalizes that each of us can be good writers. If that makes each of us special, so be it!

2. Writing Is Easy for Good Writers

A good writer, my students say, is someone who writes for enjoyment, or writes often (even when not given an assignment), as a hobby, a pastime, an avocation, or as a form of play. A good writer, they say, is someone who cannot seem to avoid writing in order to express his thoughts and feelings.

But writing for enjoyment is not the same thing as simply sitting down at the keyboard and writing a great novel. Consider the athlete who aspires to improve her game. On the practice field, she exerts herself at every opportunity, sweating and challenging herself to be better this session than before.

In the same way, one who aspires to improve his writing is often engaged in a struggle to discover what he wants to say, and how to say it just right. Good writing doesn't flow smoothly from the pen or leap from the fingers onto the computer screen. Yet the reluctant writer persists in believing he is somehow defective because his words don't come without effort.

What reluctant writers don't know is that just as athletes sweat it out in practice, so do good writers struggle with discovery and expression. Even writers who like to write don't necessarily think writing is fun. In truth, writing is work. Writing is most obviously work when the writer is trying to convey something she feels deeply and is trying to express "just right" in order to evoke a similarly strong emotion in the reader. Many attempts end in a sigh of frustration because the written words don't carry the weight of the underlying emotion, or can't quite uncover the vein of gold the writer knows lies within her heart.

I use the *five-minute sprint* (Adams 1999) to introduce students to the notion that anyone can write on demand, without a preconceived notion of what they're going to say, and that the challenge of writing can begin as fun if we remove expectations on performance.

The five-minute sprint is a main ingredient in any writer's cupboard. Instructions are simple: write fast and hard, keep the pen moving, write whatever comes to mind, and stop at the end of five minutes. Adams's instruction to "go deeper" is always useful, as is the encouragement to be fearless and to disregard concerns about spelling, handwriting, and the like.

"I didn't know I could write so much in such a short time," Natalie remarked after this process. "It doesn't make a lot of sense, but I wrote three paragraphs!"

Kathy shared, "My write veered off on something that happened yesterday. I didn't know it was still bothering me. I thought I'd got over it, but now I see I'm still mad."

For Jason, this process revealed that even repeating the same phrase (*I can't think of anything to write, I can't think of anything to write*) finally breaks open and leads to new words.

3. I Need to Know What I Want to Say Before I Begin Writing

This erroneous belief is understandable when we consider that the writing we come across as readers is a finished product. As readers, we are consumers of someone else's words. We encounter the end result. The actual process that produced a piece of writing remains hidden.

Writing takes guts. The very act of setting down words reveals to us what we want to express, even when we don't know what that is. In only a few minutes we may discover something that was previously hidden, denied, unacknowledged, or even unknown. Experienced writers know this.

After Kathy's sprint, I offered her a follow-on journal assignment: Write about what caused her to be angry the day before. I challenged her to be as honest as she could, knowing that she would never have to share what she wrote, and she could even destroy it if she wanted. I invited her to layer down to the deepest reason for her anger, perhaps using a phrase such as *And I'm also really mad about* . . . I suggested that if she didn't feel better after writing, she could move on to other activities and revisit her writing the following day.

It's important here to mention that *writing itself* is the action to take. This process can put her more in touch with her own feelings without endangering her through taking action she might regret. I tell my students that writing itself is not dangerous, but it is powerful, and it can lead us to unexpected realizations.

Writing is a tool used not just to express what one knows, but to explore what is not yet known. The authentic writer must be willing to go where the work takes him. Real writers display courage whenever they sit down to unwrap their feelings or share a life event. On the emotional side, such writing can reveal previously hidden feelings and suggest options to take. Contemplating an array of actions before taking any single one is itself empowering, and sometimes just the clarification that comes from self-expression makes further overt action unnecessary or irrelevant.

4. You Have to Suffer to Be a Good Writer

Living in a lonely, grubby attic, a slave to addiction and vice, the mythic writer struggles in solitude and squalor. How can any mere student achieve such isolation and misery? And how could her writing ever reach the creative heights to which only those who have wallowed in the depths can achieve?

As a lifelong fan of mystery novels, I'm well aware of how sin, depravity, violence, and mayhem can converge to tell a good story, but real life is much less spectacular. Still, best sellers and hit movies frequently tell tales of malevolence. Ordinary life, by comparison, is, well, ordinary.

But the world of expressive writing is full of ordinary moments, events, and objects made larger than life through the loving touch of language. We can help students appreciate the small details of daily life as well as transform their own writing by selecting examples that illuminate the beauty of specific, normal, overlooked things.

Encouraging students to write with appreciation for the smallest details and fleeting pleasant moments of their lives may actually have profound physical and mental health benefits. Recent research on human brain activity reveals that the thoughts we think, the language we use, and the attitudes we hold form firing patterns in our brains that, through repetition, create pathways along our neurons that are habitual, and that these patterns can be changed dramatically by changing our thoughts.

The structure and the very function of our brains can be changed by the way we think, and recent studies in this science of neuroplasticity show that even our genes can be turned on or off by thought. Our genes actually can be regulated by our environment, which means that a background of deprivation or trauma, or surroundings that inspire and encourage, can have lasting impact upon our lives (Doidge 2006)

Studies of contemplative practices have also shown that behavioral interventions can be "neuronally inspired," and that "thoughts can produce more targeted and specific changes in the brain than any medication" (Davidson 2009). These findings have produced significant advancements in the treatment of post-traumatic stress disorder, obsessive-compulsive disorder, and even autism.

Brain science is at last providing us with evidence that the use of affirmations, "talk therapy" interventions, meditation practices, and carefully selected writing exercises can help overcome trauma, strengthen resiliency, and improve or perhaps even prevent physical and mental illness.

According to these theories, Carlos was perhaps actually strengthening areas of his own brain related to feelings of safety and self-acceptance when he wrote this poem in class:

Sitting on the embarcadero with my father are the fondest memories that I have
It was just him and I chatting the day away while sharing a snack
Feeling safe and secure enjoying every moment
You think to yourself this time in your life will always remain and won't ever pass by

Watching the waves and seagulls diving into the cold bay for lunch
The sun's rays beating down on the barnacle covered boats
The sun is so welcoming and warms our backs
Dad is giving me advice and we are sharing stories
Ah, yes these are the moments

Follow-on assignments might include writing down the advice his father gave and capturing more shared moments in poetry or prose.

Not only does someone not have to suffer to be a good writer, but writing can actually serve to alleviate or even prevent suffering.

Susan came to the writing group one day feeling sad, remembering her father who had died several years before. I suggested she write an *unsent letter* (a letter in which one can say anything at all, even things one normally wouldn't say, because the letter won't be sent and/or because the addressee is not available) to her father, telling him her feelings of sorrow.

She wrote how she had seen a book in the window of a bookstore, written by an author they had both enjoyed, and it brought tears to her eyes. She wrote, "And remember your old green sweater? It's missing some buttons, but I wear it still."

For homework, I suggested she try writing her father's reply, imagining what he might write back in response to her memories. The next week she came in eager to share. Her father's letter ended with words of encouragement and love: "Yes, I do remember that sweater. It was my favorite. When you wear it, think of me and know that my love always surrounds you."

While one does not need to suffer to be a good writer, the reality is that many students have experienced the darker side of life. David wrote:

Imagine being in a place where it is always noisy, with shouting, swearing, and constant banging; where the lights never go off so you can sleep calmly; a place that stinks of piss and sweat and vomit. That's the prison where I lived for four years. And it's where I met the Dalai Lama.

The meeting happened, of course, through books, and David's vivid recollections brought his classmates into the presence of his previous world and helped them understand why college was so important to him.

Shelly wrote about her sister's death when they were both children, a loss that was still traumatic for her. I suggested she review her entry at home and write a reflection about it, and she later reported that she decided to reread the pages by typing them up "as if I were a third party and not someone involved." She noticed vast changes in her handwriting throughout the piece, and judged herself "pretty whacked out" because of that. After typing the entries, however, she did feel more distance. "I was surprised that I had used so many positive words in my writing. I can see now there were benefits, and that kind of surprised me, too, because I've always felt so depressed about it."

No, it isn't necessary to have suffered greatly in order to write. Hope, joy, and love can be equally powerful catalysts. However, if one has suffered, the writing process can help assuage emotional responses to difficulty.

5. Telling the Truth Is Dangerous

Although it may seem obvious that the first audience for most expressive writing is oneself, lurking underneath that first layer are less obvious layers of listeners. Reluctant writers are often hesitant because they fear that unknown adversaries are reading over their shoulders, ready to challenge and discount the writers' truths with critical and shaming judgments. This can be an especially powerful inhibitor; most writers suffer from this self-consciousness to a greater or lesser degree.

Baldwin reminds us that "very few things in life are empirically true. Events are true . . . but none of the feelings attached to such events are *the truth* about them" (1976, 50). It is the *emotional truth* of our lives that animates writing and that resonates with the reader and brings a nod of the head, an upbeat of the heart.

A writing barrier can be caused by one's own fear of what she may find out about herself through honest writing. Baldwin (1976) mentions that a desire for secrecy in writing frequently stems from our wish to remain hidden from ourselves. Thus, the urge to censor before or during writing may come not from the fear of an external critic as much as from a desire to keep ourselves unaware of a part of our lives—actions, beliefs, inconsistencies, trespasses—that we don't wish to accept. Students may project this inner critic onto their teacher and fear a poor grade or a harsh criticism as a displaced desire to remain unaware of some part of their own personalities. They may unconsciously fear a parent or other authority figure will discover their "true selves" if they write honestly.

Many writing textbooks do mention a distinction between the writer and the critic. I tell my students that during the writing process, the critic should be locked out of the room. In her book *Bird by Bird* (1994), Anne Lamott tackles the critic with her technique of *the [lousy] first draft*, sometimes called by composition teachers *prewriting* or *the zero draft*. In any case, students should be reminded that their early efforts are more like brainstorming, and nowhere near finished essays or poems, and that they can use the writing process to discover what they think and feel rather than waiting until their ideas are fully conscious and in final form before they begin to write them down.

6. Using a Thesaurus or a Rhyming Dictionary Is Cheating

Students usually agree that "real writers" carry a comprehensive lexicon in their heads, can conjure a list of synonyms in a wink, and even know a word that rhymes with *orange*. Anyone lacking these gifts is certainly doomed, since "everyone knows" that using tools like a dictionary, thesaurus, or the Internet to help locate just the right word or phrase is somehow "cheating."

This is a relatively easy myth to discredit. Every classroom, not only those dedicated to composition, should have a good dictionary, a thesaurus, and other reference books in plain sight. In the era of electronic resources, it takes only a moment to search online for derivations of words and expressions. Becoming "word sleuths" is a rewarding enterprise for students.

An interesting homework assignment could come through brainstorming some common clichés or contemporary slang terms, then sending students out on an Internet scavenger hunt to find the historical sources and explanations of them.

7. Asking Someone Else for Help Is Forbidden

An antidote to this mistaken idea is helping students share early drafts of their writing, with feedback on what stands out as interesting and evocative and what would benefit from further development. When students are close to their subjects, they may hopscotch over details that others need and would enjoy. Helpful feedback can include a response to those places where the audience asks for more: more explanation, more examples, more detail.

Using this approach, students can achieve a type of collaborative writing. Working in pairs, students read to one another a piece of writing—two or three paragraphs, or a drafted poem—on which they would like feedback. Listeners restrict comments to what they liked, found most interesting, or/ and wanted to know more about. After this initial sharing, each revises the written work, and the process is repeated. After the second revision, the work can be shared within the larger group (Fox 1995).

Collaborative writing done by a whole group is also an approach that can be used in the classroom. A group poem can be composed on a topic by having each student add one line to the growing body. A community college class wrote the following poem from the given phrase "I am thirsty for . . ."

I am thirsty for life, for knowledge.
I'm thirsty for excitement, love, laughter.
I'm thirsty for a successful life, and—
beer!

The freedom that everyone should enjoy.
I am thirsty for all the experience
that will fill the cup of my soul.

. . . the gentleness of butterfly wings
through my heart, reminding me
how fragile I am.

Inspiration in new forms.
Knowledge.
Knowledge.

I am thirsting for the renewing waters of the Holy Spirit.
A steamy cup of cocoa topped with whipped cream.

The cup of peacefulness.

Whenever my students create a group poem, I bring it in the next week typed out and copied for each class member. They are always surprised and proud of their creative accomplishment.

8. I Have to Be Good at Spelling and Grammar

Students' definitions of writing frequently contain references to good grammar, proper spelling, even neatness of handwriting. But authentic writing emerges by way of a messy process. Whether handwritten or composed on a keyboard, early drafts are anything but neat. Typos, wrong or weak word choices, sentence fragments, and other flaws should be expected. Every writing teacher knows that evoking the critic too early results in stunted products and "writers' block."

Biographies of famous writers are useful tools. Facsimile pages of early manuscript drafts are wonderful examples of how writers work, and rework, their magic. In the short film, "The Life of the Poem," William Stafford discussed how he worked. Journal entries, reflection on his process, and close-ups of his handwritten drafts reveal to the viewer how a writer considers and composes.

Cambridge University Press has published a facsimile of the entire original manuscript of Charles Dickens's *Great Expectations*. An article about the book, published online by *The Guardian*, tells how the manuscript shows Dickens's terrible handwriting, how his lines sloped down to the right and how he would squeeze a few extra words into the space this left at the bottom of a page . . . Ink-splodged and messy, the manuscript shows how Dickens was constantly returning to his text to cross out and alter sentences, also including occasional instructions to his typesetter. (Flood 2012)

We can even challenge our students to write as messily as famous writers do in order to help them overcome a tendency to neatness in early drafts.

The variety and number of writing exercises we can use in the classroom is limited only by imaginations—our own, and our students'. Any reluctant writer can be coaxed into the process with encouragement, deferred judgment, and modeling acceptance of whatever may come from her pen.

Writing is a vehicle for self-discovery as much as it is one of communication. The creative person's struggle is frequently the artful wrestling of his medium to manipulate it into expressing what he wishes to convey. Sometimes the writer knows just what he wants to say but hasn't quite achieved the skill to say it. At least as often, however, the writer doesn't really know what he wants to say until the written words reveal what has been hidden within.

Perhaps the most powerful mystery of writing is that through grappling with what we know of language, we can actually work our way into discovering something we didn't know when we began. Our very words then become the path by which we venture into our own unknown selves.

References

Adams, Kathleen. 1999. Writing as therapy. *Counseling and Human Development* 31: 5.

Baldwin, Christina. 1976. *One to one: Self-understanding through journal writing.* New York: M. Evans and Company.

Davidson, Richard J. 2009. Transform your mind, change your brain: Neuroplasticity and personal transformation," September 23, 2009. http://www. youtube.com/watch?v=7tRdDqXgsJ0. Accessed August 25, 2012.

Doidge, Norman, MD. 2006. *The brain that changes itself.* New York: Penguin Books (USA) Inc.

Flood, Alison. 2011. Dickens manuscript illuminates author's workings. *The Guardian.* http://www.guardian.co.uk/books/2011/dec/08/dickens-manuscript-great-expectations. Accessed August 25, 2012.

Fox, John. 1995. *Finding what you didn't lose.* New York: Jeremy Tarcher/Putnam.

Lamott, Anne. 1994. *Bird by bird.* New York: Anchor Books.

Acknowledgements

I wish to acknowledge the following poets and friends for the exercises and inspiration they have shared:

Kathleen Adams, for Five-Minute Sprint and List of Things I Love

Sara Jameson, senior instructor and assistant director of writing at Oregon State University for cliches and derivation hunts

Drew Myron, writer, editor, business woman, for Box of Smells

Paulann Petersen, Oregon poet laureate, for the usage of specific word lists and details

Clemens Starck, Oregon poet, for Box of Found Objects

Additional Recommended Resources

Goldberg, Natalie. 1986. *Writing down the bones: Freeing the writer within.* Boston: Shambhala Publications.

Hanson, Rick, with Richard Mendius, MD. 2009. *Buddha's brain: The practical neuroscience of happiness, love and wisdom.* Oakland: New Harbinger Publications, Inc.

Wooldridge, Susan Goldsmith. 1996. *Poemcrazy: Freeing your life with words.* New York: Three Rivers Press.

Suggested Classroom Exercises

Get Specific

Read this list of words and add some specifics of your own. Create at least two more categories in the spaces provided, and fill them with your own lists of particular words.

Box of Smells

The teacher creates a collection of small bottles or containers, putting into each a sample amount of liquid or dry (powdered) substances, each with a distinct aroma. Prior to the writing exercise, each student selects a bottle at

Table 6.1. "Get Specific" Word Lists

Trees	Flowers	Food
weeping willow	tulip	lasagna
oak	rose	peanut butter/jelly
aspen	lilac	pancakes
dogwood	lily of the valley	enchilada
maple	iris	hamburger
cottonwood	peony	broccoli
lodgepole pine	poppy	cinnamon
redwood	daisy	macaroni/cheese
___	___	___
___	___	___
___	___	___

Activities	Your own list	Your own list
tennis	___	___
horseback riding	___	___
water skiing	___	___
basketball	___	___
shuffleboard	___	___
ping pong	___	___
hiking	___	___
swimming	___	___
___	___	___
___	___	___
___	___	___

random. Once the directions for the writing exercise are given, students open their bottles, take in the smell released, and use their associations to the aroma in their writing.

Writing exercises can be structured or free flowing. The Box of Smells can be used in combination with other exercises in this chapter.

Table 6.2 has suggestions for substances that could be included in your special Box of Smells. Use your imagination to create this collection. Check it from time to time in case the samples evaporate or spoil.

Table 6.2. Box of Smells

laundry detergent	chili powder	witch hazel
fabric softener	cardamom	shampoo
dishwashing soap	ground ginger	body lotion
cinnamon	soy sauce	men's aftershave
baby powder	tea leaves	olive oil
ground cloves	tobacco	mouthwash
toothpaste	ground coffee	chocolate

Box of Found Objects

As the name suggests, this box will contain items collected from anywhere and everywhere. The more obscure or ambiguous the object is, and the more substantial and permanent it is, the better. You can also include things that might not be indestructible, and if so you may choose to have a box-within-a-box for the more fragile items.

Here are a few ideas. Use your imagination, and start collecting!

- chunks of broken electronics (beware of sharp edges)
- knobs and drawer pulls
- antique tools
- horseshoe nails
- unusual seashells

Variation

Create a collection of six to eight items with different textures. Pass these around in a closed container (paper bag or shoebox) and have students touch them without looking. Or have each student withdraw an item to use in a writing assignment. (See Table 6.3).

An item can be described as exactly as possible, or it can be used as one "person" in a dialog, a metaphor for an emotion, or any other creative application.

Table 6.3.   Textures

pine cone	cotton ball	sandpaper
piece of velvet	river stone	leather
tile	soapstone	corduroy

Word List

Students can compile their own lists, generating random words or by being given a topic such a colors, modes of transportation, or emotions.

Word lists can be used in numerous ways. Students can be instructed to write a poem containing six words chosen from the list; write an alphapoem using any single word; or write a paragraph using two words that do not apparently relate (like "apple" and "necklace"). Here are some words to start with.

Table 6.4.   Word Lists

house	jungle	dust
hammer	horse	box
dust	stairway	housefly
shoebox	thrilling	cheerful
football	boat	chasm
station wagon	skis	necklace
jacket	yellow	argument
sweater	chair	teal
quarter	blueberries	road
river	labyrinth	excitement
kitten	smile	rice
skipping	apple	money

7

Poetry and Emotional Intelligence

PERIE LONGO

Come words
Show yourself off
Show others what you're made of
Make my tongue wiggle like a snake
Make my eyes tremble
Make my ears open wide
Make my nose start smelling you
Make my fingers touch you
Let my words mean something to others
Make me happy.
—Sean Flood, grade 4[1]

When I was a child of seven, riding in the back seat of our old Chevy as we trekked into the Rocky Mountains, my father said with a voice of awe, "I think those mountains are God's necklace." My father was a zoology professor, and he wrote poetry. My mother was in the front seat. My grandma, who we were visiting and who loved the mountains almost as much as God, was next to me. She squeezed my hand. My little brother wiggled on the other side of her. It was the first time I remember chills running up my spine. My father's words were the most beautiful I had ever heard, and I wrote them down in my notebook. I suddenly had a concept of God I never had before. *God must be really big, then. And if the mountains are His necklace, His head must be the sky.* My father's words made me happy and revealed something to me I would not have found in a book at that age.

Fast forward. Now I am a poet, poetry therapist, and licensed marriage and family therapist. I have been teaching poetry writing to children from grades kindergarten through twelve for twenty-eight years. I never planned on this last part.

In 1985, a poet friend who taught in the California Poets in the Schools program had contracted to teach four sessions in two second-grade classes. She suddenly had been hired to teach English full time in another state, starting immediately, and pressed me to take the classes. I was teaching speech at our local community college and was not at all interested. "I can't teach children," I insisted. She persisted.

I finally agreed, but only if she prepared me. She handed me a copy of Kenneth Koch's *Wishes, Lies and Dreams* (1970) and left town. I haven't seen her since.

A week later I went into the second grade, opened Koch's chapter on metaphor, and read to them, "Your nose is a banana except it isn't yellow." Actually, the line is written, "A nose is a banana except it is Yellow" (146), but I was nervous and forgot to put on my reading glasses. The children thought it was the funniest thing they ever heard! An adult coming in and saying such a thing!

I made up another silly example to hear them laugh again. "My hair is spaghetti but it isn't red with tomatoes." More hilarity. Then it was their turn to say something not true about me. "Your mouth is a strawberry but it doesn't have a stem." After several offerings, writing paper was hurriedly handed out. They had ten minutes, I told them, to write similar lines about themselves or their parents, friends, and teachers. The two rules were not to rhyme and to have fun with words without hurting anyone's feelings.

I did not know that some of them could barely write, some had poor language skills, and most were used to filling in blanks on worksheets. When the students asked me how to spell this or that, I said to sound it out as best as they could, because we can't be creative and correct things at the same time. I played the same soft music that I like to listen to when I write, to get beyond judgment of whether the writing is "good."

I had never been so amazed in a classroom. Their enthusiasm was contagious. Most of them wrote something, read to peals of laughter, and asked when I could come again. Of course, I came the next three weeks.

As the holidays approached I had the students write poems in their favorite holiday shapes such as a wreath, candle, star, or tree. They were to do "comparisons" (an easier word than *similes*) for the thing they wrote about. I explained how a cookie or a wreath was the shape of the world that we are all a part of, which makes us very special, and when we write poetry, it tells us things we don't know we know. A little boy named Matt wrote, "A circle can't do nothin'/ cut in half." The intelligence behind that is astounding for an eight-year-old.

Every child is a natural poet, and "poetry is a circle of experience sculpted on the page that brings a child to the magic of self" (Longo 1985, 69). The symbolism of the circle allowed little Matt to describe his experience, whatever it was, and to give all of us something to ponder the rest of our lives. I still see the look in his eyes when he gave me his poem with a hole in it where he'd erased a word and put another next to it, so his two-line poem could say what he felt.

Another child wrote from the bottom of the page up, "My poem goes like a tree grows." The teacher informed me he was dyslexic, and it was the first time he had ever tried to write.

The school wrote a grant to have me come and teach poetry in the rest of the grades the coming spring. Soon I was being asked to give talks and in-services about how to teach poetry to youngsters. Most teachers didn't relish the two-week required unit. Looking back, all I really knew was *your nose is a banana*, that I love poetry almost as much as I love children, and that youngsters love discovering themselves and learning ways to express their joys and sorrows through the magic of words. I also witnessed then, and continue to witness, what Robert Frost wrote—that poetry "begins in delight and ends in wisdom . . . It inclines to the impulse, it assumes direction with the first line laid down, it runs a course . . . and ends in a clarification of life" (Leedy 1985, 84). The delight I felt at my beginnings as a poetry teacher must be what children experience the first time they encounter the beauty and joy of language and the freedom to speak from their hearts through creative expression, without judgment or correction.

Poetry and Emotional Intelligence

Emotional intelligence was not a common phrase when I began, but I learned along the way that when a child is able to say how the world is for him through figurative language, image, detail, rhythm, and shape, he learns things that last a lifetime. More than a decade after those first classes, I entered a third-grade classroom for a first poetry lesson. The teacher greeted me with open arms. He told his class to listen to everything I said, and that he became a teacher because of poetry lessons he had with me back in the fifth grade. Somehow I recalled the poem he wrote about turquoise and that his favorite word was *authentic*. My memory shocked him.

Because I type a poem from each student in each class over the course of four to eight lessons, sometimes I remember such things, even if not the student's name. I put a star next to lines that are creative or imaginative examples of something we've talked about—some detail, image, or emotional description—with a note at the bottom of the page about what they have done particularly well. The students know their poems are read. They learn to listen to each other and say what they hear that makes their insides twinkle. They connect their feelings to the thoughts and images of the poets presented that inspire them to their own writing. Through creative discovery, flashes of imagination, and insight, they become more self-aware. They are able to extend that self-awareness to their classmates' poems and feel what they feel—a natural, empathic response. Self-esteem increases. So does respect, and seeds are planted for better understanding the world around them, with its confusions, paradoxes, and contradictions.

Equally important, they come to know themselves as related to and an integral part of the wider community of human beings. Poetry certainly can help set the stage for the development of empathy and empathic listening, the key to "enhancing emotional intelligence" (Gottman and DeClaire 1997, 70). The opening poem by Sean captures some of these elements. The lesson was simply "Words," using a poem by Joseph Bruchac that begins with the line, "Let my words / be bright with animals . . . " and Pat Mora's poem "Words Free as Confetti" that begins "Come, words, come in your every color." (Not long after my inauguration with noses and bananas, I learned the basic strategy of using well-chosen literature to provide images, language, and a model for technique.) For every lesson I remind students to use similes and metaphors, if possible, and to consider the five sense words (sight, sound, touch, taste, and smell) along with the sixth sense of intuition, which I define for them as "what the poem tells you that you didn't know you knew." Note how Sean's poem integrates these two concepts and then how he leaps to "Let my words mean something to others," suggesting his longing to connect with others, which would make him happy. He looks inward in delight and looks outward in wisdom.

Another poem written during that same class is so different, as every child's poem is. What stands out to me is the sophistication of an emotionally intelligent child with his imaginative imagery, the music of the language, the sounds of the words, and the unconscious "knowing" that would carry his soul to unknown places.

The Garden of Bliss
If I had a garden full of life
it would have a waterfall with words
instead of water.
I would have a purple dog circling
over the lake of tears and the grass,
oh the long green grass slowly swinging
gently through the breeze as little creatures
carry my soul to different places
that no man has ever gone. The sheets
of snow glistening like a garden full
of glass and a sleek black cat walking
through the white snow.
—Morgan Thornley, grade 4

How I Teach Poetry to Children

My first California Poets in the Schools (CPITS) fall conference was held deep in the northern California redwoods on the edge of the Russian River. It was two days of constant rain; water dripping through holes in our sleeping tents, soaking our papers and us. But I had the pleasure of meeting poets from around the state as I attended workshops and gathered the outpouring of poems, lesson plans, and sources. One problem was that the river had risen along with my knowledge, and we almost couldn't make it back across the bridge! That first conference "bridged" me into this new and wonderful work in ways that continue to serve me.

CPITS began in 1964 at San Francisco State University with funding from the California Arts Council and the National Endowment for the Arts. Soon after, it expanded beyond Northern California. The purpose was to send poets of diversity into classrooms with literature that went beyond the poets most often anthologized in language arts texts and that reflected the many cultures of the children. CPITS is now the largest writers-in-schools program in the United States that is administered by local area coordinators. Since 1987, CPITS has placed a yearly average of over 150 poets in more than three hundred schools across the state to work with twenty-five thousand students in grades kindergarten through twelfth, with over one hundred thousand poems written every year.

As in all segments of education, funding has severely diminished, so today the program is made possible by private foundations, grants, and, depending on the location, even Parent-Teacher Associations. Each year CPITS publishes an anthology of student poems. All California counties are represented.

Most of the CPITS poets present a lesson in a somewhat similar way, though our styles vary as widely as our experience and backgrounds. Yet all of us have heard the questions: "How could a child write this poem? How do you do it?" Here's the basic process of how CPITS poets are trained.

- A sample poem(s) is distributed reflecting a particular theme or technique. It is best if the teacher reads the poem first, slowly and with feeling, as if it is the most important poem in the world, energizing the students to the music of the words and feeling.
- Next, have the whole class read with the teacher, perhaps dividing the class into sections. This way the students absorb the rhythm of the words.
- Then have students talk about lines or parts of the poems they like or identify with, and what memories, experiences, and feelings the poem evokes.

From student responses and the poem itself, a structure emerges of things to consider for their writing. Often the presented poem has a line or image that can be used as the starting place of the child's poem. The brainstorming that happens in response to the teacher's questions can yield structures. The teacher writes the structuring elements on the board. When the excitement peaks, it's time to write.

Even though the teacher has given a review of all that has been said and has asked if there are any final questions. Most often there are not, until they look at the blank paper. For some, this can be like looking down a steep mountain of snow on the first ski run. At least one student will then ask, "What are we writing about?" or "Do I have to do that?" This is the all-important "stall" akin to sorting the laundry or getting a snack or looking for a misplaced bill you forgot to pay.

I relax the anxiety by playing soft music in the background. I tell students to forget about writing something "good." Some classes like to turn the lights down, just as some poets, in the privacy of their writing spaces, light candles. It is all preparation to go to that special place inside, the rare solitude in a busy world where we can be in silent communication with thoughts and images, a sort of dream, a trance state that children tend to access more quickly than adults. I remind them to begin writing their name and to pick one of the line beginnings off the board. I turn on the music. Perhaps I pass around pictures from magazines for imagery and similes. I might scatter a handful of individual words on colored index cards cut in thirds. Two words, like *orange* and *dream*, can trigger a whole poem. The younger the grade, the more simple the words. Other times I write on the board words spoken during the brainstorming part of the lesson.

Suddenly, there is complete quiet except for the scratching of pencils on paper. It is amazing to witness. Stephen Spender explains it this way: "Writing poetry is a spiritual activity which makes one completely forget for the time being, that one has a body" (Spender 1952, 114). Rollo May writes that the moment of creation is one of "absorption . . . the encounter of the intensively conscious human being with his or her world" (May 1978, 56).

For elementary-age children, the writing time may last only five or ten minutes, but it is always enough. Gradually, the quicker writers come up for air, and approval, running to me with, "I'm finished. Will you read it?" I tell them I will, as soon as I help those who feel "stuck." Usually a question or two will get the stuck ones moving again. I remind them to look over their poem, add or subtract anything, and decide if they want to share or not.

Children have small voices, so it is best to have them stand in the front of the class or sit on an "author's stool" to read. It is important to talk about how nervousness is normal and why the heart flip-flops around. I talk about how we all want people to like our poem, and we don't want anyone to make fun of us. I talk about how listening well creates safety and shows respect. A poem is like a gem, a gift to treasure wrap in the bow of friendship.

After a child reads, one or two students are asked to say something that stood out to them. Peer comments promote equity, respect, and inclusion. There is such joy during these final moments of the class. If time is a little short, I will have children turn to someone near them and read their poems to each other. Writing poetry is "sustenance" to the child, Sheryl Noethe writes, "making their lives richer." It gives them "a grip on existence, an empowerment, and a way to listen to the truth of the self" (Collum and Noethe 1994, xvi).

"My Secret Place": A Demonstration

A friend once asked why I'd left college teaching to teach poetry to children. I responded that I thought it was important that children experience the place deep inside, beyond conversation, the place they can count on, where they can experience solitude and observe the world around them, the place of feelings, the place where they understand things they didn't learn in books. Carl Jung said, "Through our feelings we experience the known, but our intuitions point to things that are unknown and hidden—that by their very nature are secret" (Jung 1952, 216). I told my friend it was important to me to help children find that secret place.

That conversation caused me to develop a lesson called My Secret Place. I searched until I found the "right" two poems: "Song of the Pines" by Po Chu I (772–846) and D. H. Lawrence's "Delight of Being Alone." Po Chu's opening lines are

I like sitting alone when the moon is shining,
two pines standing before the verandah.

Lawrence describes how being alone

> *makes me realize the delicious pleasure*
> *of the moon that she has in traveling*
> *by herself, throughout time.*

As an additional teaching tool, working poets sometimes write their own poems to accompany the masters. Here is mine:

My Secret Place
My secret place is full
of cat whiskers and a snake skin
smooth as water with diamonds
on its back blazing
like freshly packed snowballs
I bat to the sun
which whistles them down
as poems shouting
> *Let me out*
> *Hurl me around the world*
> *For everyone to hear*
Weather can't make up its mind
in my secret place
full of sunshade
> *brightrain*
> *moonbows*
and child hushes piping music
through pencils   Shhhhhh
Sheep are being counted

At the time, my daughter was in the third grade. I first tried the lesson in her class. Before handing out the page of printed poems, I asked the children to raise their hands if they liked being alone. I was surprised that most hands shot up. Then I asked where they liked to go. Replies were: *bedrooms, trees and tree forts, a creek, the cubby under the staircase.* Then I asked about places they travel in their imagination. Responses were more exotic: *outer space, on top of the rainbow.* We first read the Po Chu and Lawrence poems. They noted that the moon and pine trees were mentioned in both poems and that they often looked at these same images.

Then they read my poem. Silence. I asked if anyone had any questions. One brave child said it was "weird" and asked where this place was. I confessed it was my office. I said I liked to collect things and had a tiny box of our cat, Gravity's, whiskers. Then came the snakeskin. I admitted my son found it and gave it to me; I thought it was beautiful. Internally, I wished I had brought in both the whiskers and skin. I drew the snakeskin on the board.

Then the children started talking about odd things they had in their rooms. I was asked about how the diamonds on the snakeskin could turn into snowballs. The magic question, where the imagination takes over—a riddle to be solved. They figured it out eventually, when I explained the diamonds "blazed like snowballs," which made me think of how I once heard that Octavio Paz said our poems are out there waiting for us to catch them and bring them to light on our papers.

The words *sunshade, brightrain,* and *moonbows* perplexed them at first. They quickly solved those riddles also, most having seen moonbows, and rain when the sun was out, or sat in the shade with their feet in the sun. "Some poets run words together," I explained, "like e. e. cummings, who wrote 'rustleandrun' and 'hidehidhide' in his poem 'Hist Wist' about Halloween, so I played with that idea. Does it work?" Students love to make comments on my poems, when I ask, and even make changes.

It is important to engage their minds with problem solving, to get them thinking outside of the box, to encourage creativity. The line, "Shhhhh / Sheep are being counted" always raises lots of questions and possible meanings until I ask them what it feels like right before they fall asleep. One of my favorites: "Half way gone." They figure out that it is rather like a waking-dream state. I offer that it is that stillness that overcomes them when they write poetry, beyond worry, when the unconscious raises its head.

I quote my (now thirty-six-year-old) daughter Cecily's poem. She gave her permission, and even remembers writing it. Her secret place shows how the external images are unconscious metaphors for internal feelings.

> *My secret place is*
> *where bamboo is crisp*

Wind whips the tall trees
in twists and turns

Trees grow in creeks
while leaves spin their destiny

Mud banks are cozy and warm
My secret place stays the same
in a storm

The rhyme in the last stanza is something children often do, without thinking about it. What is more noticeable is no matter what is going on externally, the child can find refuge and comfort in their inner world. Over the years I've done this lesson, the poems reveal a child's depth of thought, sense of wonder, love of nature, and the need to escape from the noise of their lives to think their own thoughts.

In first lessons, I always ask who likes poetry and who doesn't, or who likes some poems and not others. I admit to the class that there are many poems I don't enjoy because they are boring or too difficult. Right away we're on the same page. I open a book of poems and ask how a poem looks different than a story. "It's shorter." "There's lots of space." "It has a shape." From third grade on we continue making a list. "It rhymes." We discuss that a poem doesn't have to rhyme, but it does have rhythm, like a song. Poetry is like music without the melody, I tell them. It has a beat achieved through "repeats" of whole lines, phrases, words, and sounds.

They look at the poems handed out and offer examples of any repetitions they notice. We talk about what makes a poem boring. "When nothing happens," someone says. Poetry is the "language of the heart," I explain. We show our feelings through images, which helps make poetry exciting. Comparisons using *like* or *as* also show how we *feel* about what we are writing about.

The shape of a poem is the last item on the list. It takes a few classes for them to not fill up the whole page, margin to margin. I've found if I have them fold the paper in half to write "skinny" poems, that helps, or to draw a square or rectangle in the middle of the page and write the poem inside. They giggle at the thought that they can write inside the box in order to think outside the box. Some love to write in circles or a diamond shape.

Right away they begin to play with the concept of shape. Something happens to how they use words when space is confined. They find it helpful to learn that *poetry* comes from the Greek word *poesis*, which means "building," and *stanza* is from an Italian word meaning "room," so a stanza is a room in the house of a poem.

A side note about shape, addressed to educators and counselors, comes from my poetry therapy training and experience. When we are writing about feelings, there is an unconscious sense that we will stay in control—we won't fall off the page—if there is a container.

The sounds of words also convey feeling. Soothing vowel sounds are like a river for sadness or loneliness, and the consonants are like the banks that shore up the flow. The plosive "t's and "p's" and the sizzle of "s's" can show anger, all of these feelings in one poem. Little of this will be remembered all at once, so with each new lesson we focus on one or two of these items, and I often repeat these techniques that are at the heart of poetry since the beginning of time. I will then offer a definition of poetry: *A way of giving sound, sense, and shape to the silence within.*

Expressive Writing in Difficult Times

One of the benefits of children becoming comfortable with writing poetry is this: When something terrible happens before their eyes, they have a tool to process it effectively. Poetry is a way to cope with trauma. The emotionally intelligent child may be afraid of what is happening outside of herself, but she is not afraid to go inside to write about it. Over the years, there have been a few times when I've walked into a classroom and what I'd planned was set aside because of what the children were experiencing.

January 28, 1986, was one of those times. As I was getting ready to leave for class, the morning news was full of the *Challenger* liftoff; suddenly there was a commotion on the television. A twisting swirl of smoke appeared in the clear, blue sky. The *Challenger* had exploded. I watched in horror, trembling. All seven astronauts were killed. I had to leave. Everything was split in two. I wondered how I could teach. When I walked into the classroom, the children were watching the *Challenger* disintegrate on the television. It looked like an alien beast with two tentacles roaming over the atmosphere looking for a place to land. The teacher turned off the television. I asked for any phrases or words that came to their mind. "It was a perfect morning." "Blue sky." "Everything changed." I told them to give their feelings an image. "Put your head in your heart . . . list details . . . we can't make sense of it . . . write in jerks . . . write as if you were one of the people on board." A little boy accepted the challenge, and his poem was published in the CPITS anthology that year.

A Pilot's Point
My stomach is queasy
as if this is my last meal
but I am determined
It is the calm
before the storm

Goodbye
LIFT OFF

My heart is intense as
I go now
a starchild to be reborn
—in Longo 1986, 74–75

This fourth-grader found a way to transform the horror into an image to comfort himself. As he read, I saw his whole body relax. His classmates sighed. They didn't even hear the recess bell ring as more shared their poems, not making sense of the event but expressing their deepest feelings.

In 1991, the United States intervened to help liberate Kuwait from Iraq. That evening, the television showed haunting images of explosions and destruction. The next morning I had a class with second-graders. The children were buzzing with fear that something terrible might happen to them, that war would also start here. I asked if they wanted to write about it. They did. The following poem was published in the 1991 CPITS anthology.

The Sky Watches
the sky watches in sadness in worry in pain
the greed the hate for tonight there may be war
the seagulls cry and fly away
there is sadness spread over the world
you do not know love but hate
for in your heart you're afraid and hurt
do not run from your life and the sadness
you are making in it
you have a choice stop
—Naomi A. Miller-Wave, grade 2 (in CPITS 1991, 7)

Naomi did not understand the politics or the reason for the war, only that she did not want to see people killed, which is the wish of any child. For one so young to have these words rise from her unconscious is a powerful example of how writing poetry can help in a very confusing time. If she wrote it, someone would listen, something would change. Her last line shows she had developed the confidence that her words would matter. When she read to the class, I responded, "I can hear how afraid you are that something might happen to you." I didn't say "don't worry," or "you'll be fine." By writing about the war, she had a chance to confront her own fear, and the class responded with theirs. Immediately a calm descended, and they went out to recess to play in the sun.

These are extraordinary circumstances, too often present in children's lives, but the stress and tension of daily life is also unnerving, though far more subtly, and this stress shows up in their poems in meaningful ways. One such stress is testing, a sore subject for teachers who are required to "teach to the test," as well as for students. The following poem, by a fourth grader, was written during a lesson focused on expressing strong feelings.

Testing
Oh testing, oh testing how it makes
me go crazy. It drives me bananas. It goes
as fast as a race car. When I tell it to stop
it says, "No! more more more."
But test, I want to be as free as a fox.

I want to swim in the ocean.
I want to fly like a bird.
I want
to be
free,
free.
I wish this
world can have
world peace. That is
what the world needs.
The students say, NO test!
I don't like it but the teacher
says it helps your life and
it makes you a better person.
—Isabella Robarge, grade 4

We laugh at the last line, at the same time understanding her frustration and the serious truth of what she is facing, along with expressing that the test is failing her needs. Her last line reminds me of a comment by Ted Kooser, 2004 U.S. poet laureate: "I'd like a world, wouldn't you, in which people actually took time to think about what they were saying? It would be, I'm certain, a more peaceful, more reasonable place" (2005, 5). He continues, quoting poet Seamus Heaney: "The aim of the poet and the poetry is finally to be of service, to ply the effort of the individual work into the larger work of the community as a whole" (6).

Parents and educators know that for their children, what makes for a "better person" is not a test, but an environment of love, understanding, communication, validation, enriching opportunities, and feeling that they matter. In school, the arts have a paramount place of importance, along with sports, yet the arts are always the first to be cut or dismissed as unimportant. This year, the grant for the poetry program at one of my schools was denied in favor of technology. In today's world, that is certainly important, but over thirty years ago, psychologist Rollo May wrote:

To the extent that we lose this free, original creativity of the spirit as it is exemplified in poetry and music and art, we shall lose our scientific creativity.

Scientists themselves, particularly physicists, have told us that the creativity of science is bound up with the freedom of human beings to create in the free, pure sense. (1978, 77)

To that extent, I am privileged to do my part as a poet in the community, to give to children the opportunity to develop their emotional intelligence through creativity. During the third session of a four-session poetry workshop, a child came up to me and asked if she could write about divorce. "Lots of children suffer from this," she said wide-eyed, "and I have something I want to say." The lesson was on exaggerations, which we need to do sometimes to get people to pay attention. Of course, I supported her in writing whatever she wanted.

Divorce
Divorce is a painful thing to deal with.
When bad things happen between your parents,

it affects your life, their life, your family's life.
It feels like a heavy stone weighing you down

on the cold floor, breaking you

into pieces. Every feeling so strong

and powerful. Sometimes your parents take turns
and sometimes you're separated from one parent
and always with the other.

Divorce brings sadness but one day
you must let the pain flow behind you.

I know it's hard, but you must let go
to go on with your life.
—Lea Robins, grade 5 (2012, 69)

Lea was a shy child. She did not want to read to the class at the moment of writing, but said she would share with her good friends, and I know she shared the poem with her teacher and mother. When I read it, I quietly said I could feel in her poem how hard divorce had been for her, and I also heard she had learned something very important. She smiled and skipped away. What was said between the lines of the poem is easy for all of us to understand.

Three More Lessons

Lea's wise words beyond her years at the end of her poem, *You must let go / to go on with your life,* remind me of an article by Robert Anderson, *The Magic of Metaphor: Children Writing Poetry in the Nuclear Age* (1985), that I read while researching my dissertation:

> Considered concurrently, messages from psychologists, philosophers, poets and brain scientists affirm that persons are already poetry, and need not "choose" to try to be so . . . the mind is inherently poetic. Personal growth is therefore a non-task. It is not achieved through increased effort and trying to grow, but is a letting-go of assumptions which block this awareness. (Anderson, 35)

My experience has shown this is as true for children as well as adults. The essence of creativity is giving oneself over to the process of discovery. Each time I enter a classroom, I must let go of any expectations of what children will write, or that they will write, or pay attention to any structure I scribble on the board. What always surprises me is how poetic they are by nature. However, if I do not put a structure or ideas on the board, they don't know where to begin.

As we review the prompts and possibilities, more than one child will ask, "Do I have to do that?" The answer is always, "No. Do what your heart and pencil want. You are the boss of your poem." Left to their own devices, when their creativity and feelings have been valued and they have been taught a few tools of figurative language, they tackle the task of writing poetry with little or no trouble, great joy, and play.

Goleman writes, "The emotional mind is far quicker than the rational mind, springing into action without pausing even a moment to consider what it is doing" (1997, 291). Teachers can take heart that it is easier for children to write poetry than for most adults, and that if you have spare minutes, or a rainy day, writing poetry is a worthwhile, pleasant activity. Some teachers have "Poet Trees" in their classrooms, where poems are pinned on the branches, sometimes anonymously, for all to read quietly.

At the end of this chapter are resources that are packed with ideas, including the CPITS annual anthologies with poems by children in grades K–12, which can inspire many children to grab their pencils and write. U.S. poet laureate and educator Philip Levine wrote in the 2007 CPITS anthology, *My Song Is the Light*:

> With really young poets the proper teaching strategy is immediately obvious: Get out of their way. Show them or read them poems that sing or present vivid images, or puzzle their minds into thoughts they never had before . . . they are far closer to the truth that poetry—like all the arts—is a form of play. (15)

Of the many lessons I have brought to children over the years, I choose three here with specific examples to demonstrate how the emotional mind of the young writer takes over when given free rein.

If You Walked into My Heart You Would See

"If You Walked into My Heart You Would See" is an excellent way to help children value their life as poetic, an idea originally shared by CPITS poet Eve Poole-Gilson. I read a couple of student samples, and mine, which ends:

> *If you swam inside my heart, you'd see yourself*
> *writing about what fills your heart,*
> *your poems the hope of the world and*
> *we would be strangers no longer.*

The children themselves suggest beginning with other phrases like "dive into," "skateboard into," but not "look into." That is too ordinary, too linear. If they begin with a strong verb they identify with, something magical happens. The direction is to pack into a poem things they love: people, sports, activities, weather, images from nature, pets, and memories—a sort of list poem. We then write a group poem on the board that engages all of their senses and personal experiences. I remind them of perhaps only one rule: to use images and similes.

Mike went with his own flow, not using any ideas on the board, but he created a sort of fantasy place. If you truly did enter his heart, you would live in his imagination, for him the perfect world.

The Hole in My Heart
If you walked into my heart
you would find very tall mountains
so it's very hard to get into it.
But there would be a hole in one
of the mountains so you could
get through. Once you're in
you can never get out because
the hole would close and you would
never be hungry or thirsty
and you would never age.
If you are a baby you would be a baby
for the rest of your life.
But you would never be bored
you would always be happy
you would never be tired
and if you want to you can just
sit somewhere and stare.
—Mike Marzio, grade 4

The last lines capture, for me, the moment both Spender and May described earlier in this chapter, that state of absorption when creativity takes hold, the "secret place," and the compassion of a child who connects with all ages of people, wanting the best for everyone, and especially to just be mindful, "sit somewhere and stare," be in the moment, a catalyst for all creativity.

The Unwritten

This lesson is designed to help children articulate grief and to speak into a poem something that they have a hard time expressing.

Some years ago I wrote a poem titled "The Unwritten," inspired by a poem of the same title by W. S. Merwin which begins with the lines

How come no one writes about froth
on top of cappuccino like the wave's foam
that sizzles in your ear

There are many playful images, like "the jingle of keys," "starfish tentacles like violin strings," but the last lines address loss.

What about the hug that draws you back
into yourself after a hard day,
how good it feels like the word thanks
unlike death that weights the tongue.
No one likes to mention how some people
disappear like a fast ball over the fence
leaving your eyes pasted on the sky
looking for some sign they made it home.

I ask what images and lines speak to them. Where do they find themselves in the poem? What do they think about the last lines? The children start talking about things they've never written about, or read about, or things that are hard to discuss. They will ask if I knew someone who died, and I tell them my husband did. I will ask if they know anyone who has died. Every hand pops up. Children hold on to grief. If unexpressed, this can have unfortunate consequences over time, the least of which is acting-out behavior. Often this poem gives them an opportunity to reveal the sadness they carry in their hearts, as in Lea's poem about divorce, and in the following poem.

I've Never Written About (excerpt)
I've never written about my future
and who I will become. Sometimes I wonder

where I'll live and how I will live.
I want to live with my brother.
I've never written about him.
His smiling face and big body
to put my arms around.
I could go on and on. . . .

When I miss my brother, he tells me
to look up and he'll be there. I know
that's the truth. That's what I want to believe.
Hours pass. The sky becomes dark.
Stars shimmer and shine like silver earrings.
The moon comes out and lights up the ground
so I can see where I am. This is where
I want to be.
—Ruby Tara Singh, grade 6

Ruby didn't bother with the suggestions on the board to start with interesting poetic images or using similes. She simply wrote what was in her heart. Goleman says "that the crucial emotional competencies can indeed be learned and improved upon by children—if we bother to teach them" (1997, 34). This poem to me is a stunning example of that and one of the key characteristics of the emotionally intelligent child, "to regulate one's moods and keep distress from swamping the ability to think" (34). She arrives at a resolution through a developed ability to look her grief in the face. The dark is lit up with the stars and moon so she "can see where I am," a metaphor to show how, even though she misses her brother, she hears him from far away, and how he is brought close to her through the comfort of her poem.

"Every Time I Write a Poem, I Fall in Love with It"

At the close of my four-to-six-week residencies, I often have children write about poetry and do evaluations. Some of my favorite lines from their comments are "Poetry is better than Disneyland," and "Every time I write a poem I fall in love with it." A seventh grader once wrote, "If all writing is a picnic basket, then poetry is the chocolate cake."

I read these quotes and perhaps two other poems written by children on the subject, along with the line from Pablo Neruda's poem "Poetry," which says his "heart broke loose on the wind" when he began writing. We discuss what that means. Some of their replies are humorous, such as "his heart must be like a kite" or "Where did it land?" Some emotionally bright child will get it, that the poet's heart opened to everything beautiful. A third-grader wrote some years ago that poetry is "like lightning," and goes on—

People gathering as much as they can
giving it to their grandchildren
who give it on and on
spreading it all over the world.

I share my poem titled "My Tasty Poem."

My poem tastes like the sun and moon
and stars all mixed together.
My poem wakes up bears from
their long sleep and they come out
growling for words, happy words
like jumble and tumble,
hungry words like blueberry pancakes
with honey syrup. My poem takes away
your hunger, scatters peace all over
the globe. It gladdens your heart
forever and is full of hope.

We brainstorm ideas and write them on the board about what their poem tastes like, what magic it can do, what its favorite words are, what it is about, and what wish it might have. This year fourth-grader Naomi Buchmiller wrote:

The Best Moment of My Life
When I'm doing poetry, I feel . . .

I feel . . . What's the word? . . . Peaceful,
happy; I feel like the world has escaped
from my grasp. All my worries have flown
to another universe, but they always
come back sometime. My pencil floats
to write all the words it is writing now.
A volcano erupts. I see the lava flowing down.
The world has been shrunk to the size
of my hand. I fly as high
as the sky will let me. I have confidence
that the poem will be great. Poetry, to me,
is the best moment of my life! I feel
like a starfish at the cool tidepools
in the middle of summer.
—Naomi C. Buchmiller, grade 4

Another highlight of an emotionally intelligent child, Goleman says, is to "empathize and to hope" (1997, 34). I would say another characteristic I have witnessed again and again is that traumatic events often happen in children's poems, but they transform them. In Naomi's poem "a volcano erupts," but she has control of the situation. The world shrinks into her hand, and she can make life as she wants it, peaceful, "like a starfish at the cool tidepools," the open vowel sounds conveying the deep love she feels for poetry, which is really herself. If she can accomplish this in a poem, she can also do it in the future—on the other side of the poem.

"Listen to these young poets and you'll discover the voice of the present and hear the voice of the future before the future is even here," writes Philip Levine on the CPITS website (CPITS.org). Today our children are "digital natives" in the digital age where information about everything is available at the click of a button or the slide of a finger on their iPhones and iPads. The repercussions of this are still unclear, but a 2012 *Newsweek* article asserted that technology has created an addiction of its own, increasing ADHD and OCD disorders as well as depression. "Children describe mothers and fathers unavailable in profound ways, present, and yet not there at all. . . . Technology can make us forget important things we know about life" (Dokoupil 2012, 30).

As educators, counselors, and parents, we must be all the more aware of this phenomenon and protect our children by continuing to support activities that enhance their emotional growth, even if it means "unplugging." With consistent exposure to poetry and writing, children's emotional intelligence expands. Let us hope that our children will continue to be exposed to poetry's riches and benefits between all the clicks, swipes, texts, and tweets. We owe them a brighter, more intelligent world, one where we do not fear emotion but learn to value and tender its vital expression. As Sean says in his opening poem, *Come words . . . / Make me happy.*

References

Anderson, Robert, and Kevin E. McClearey. 1984, Spring. Pointing toward a poetics of personal growth. *Revision: A Journal of Consciousness and Change.*

California Poets in the Schools. 2012. www.cpits.org, accessed July 17, 2012.

Collum, Jack, and Sheryl Noethe. 1994. *Poetry everywhere.* New York: Teachers & Writers Collaborative.

Dokoupil, Tony. 2012. Tweets, texts, email, posts: Is the onslaught making us crazy? *Newsweek*, July 16, 24–30.

Goleman, Daniel. 1997. *Emotional intelligence: Why it can matter more than IQ.* New York: Bantam.

Gottman, John, and Joan DeClaire. 1997. *Raising an emotionally intelligent child: The art of parenting.* New York: Simon and Schuster Paperbacks.

Jung, Carl. 1952. Psychology and literature. In *The creative process: A symposium.* B. Ghiselin, ed. New York: New American Library.

Koch, Kenneth. 1970. *Wishes, lies and dreams.* New York: Harper & Row.

Kooser, Ted. 2005. *The poetry home repair manual: Practical advice for beginning poets.* Lincoln: University of Nebraska Press.

Leedy, Jack J., ed. 1985. *Poetry as healer: Mending the troubled mind.* New York: Vanguard.

Levine, Philip. 2007. Forward: The question. In *My song is the light.* San Francisco, CA: California Poets in the Schools.

Longo, Perie. 1985. A circle can't do nothin' cut in half. In *Forgotten languages*. San Francisco: California Poets in the Schools.

———. 1986. Metaphor to metamorphosis. In *Under the bridge of silence*. San Francisco: California Poets in the Schools.

May, Rollo. 1978. *The courage to create*. New York: Bantam Books.

Miller-Wave, Naomi A. 1991. The sky watches. In *Remembering what happened*. San Francisco: California Poets in the Schools.

Robins, Lea. 2012. In *Turning into Stars*. San Franciso: California Poets in the Schools.

Spender, Stephen. 1952. The making of a poem. In *The creative process: A symposium*. B. Ghiselin, ed. New York: New American Library.

Teacher and Children's Sources for Writing Poetry

California Poets in the Schools. Annual anthologies. www.cpits.org.

Fletcher, Ralph. 2002. *Poetry matters: Writing a poem from the inside out*. New York: HarperCollins.

Gensler, Kinereth, and Nina Nyhart. 1978. *The poetry connection: An anthology of contemporary poets with ideas to stimulate children's writing*. New York: Teachers and Writers Collaborative.

Gordon, Ruth. 1993. *Peeling the onion: An anthology of poems*. New York: HarperCollins Childrens Books.

Heard, Georgia. 1987. *For the good of the earth and sun*. Portsmouth, NH: Heinemann.

———. 2002. *This place I know: Poems of comfort*. Somerville, MA: Candlewick Press.

Kennedy, X. J., and Dorothy Kennedy. 1982. *Knock at a star: A child's introduction to poetry*. New York: Little Brown and Company.

Koch, Kenneth. 1970. *Wishes, lies and dreams: Teaching children to write poetry*. New York: Vintage Books.

———. 1973. *Rose, where did you get that red? Teaching great poetry to children.* New York: Vintage Books.

Kowit, Steve. 1995. *In the palm of your hand.* Gardiner, ME: Tilbury House Publishers.

Montenegro, Laura Nyman. 2003. *A bird about to sing.* Boston: Houghton Mifflin Company.

National Association for Poetry Therapy. poetrytherapy.org, accessed July 17, 2012.

National Federation for Biblio/Poetry Therapy. nfbpt.com, accessed July 17, 2012.

Nye, Naomi Shihab. 1992. *This same sky: A collection of poems from around the world.* New York: Aladdin Paperbacks.

Simeon, John-Pierre, and Olivier Tallec. 2007. *This is a poem that heals fish.* New York: Enchanted Lion Books.

Statman, M. 2000. *Listener in the snow: The practice and teaching of poetry.* New York: Teachers and Writers Collaborative.

Wendt, Ingrid. 1983. *Starting with little things: A guide to writing poetry in the classroom.* Portland: Oregon Arts Foundation.

Wooldridge, Susan. 1996. *Poemcrazy: Freeing your life with words.* New York: Clarkson/Potter Publishers.

Note

1. All children's names and poems are used with permission.

8

Expressive Writing with Teens at Risk

Richard Gold

How Tucked in the Corner
Dedicated to my mom

You see that I'm alone
You see that I steal
But you don't know me.

You would know me if
You knew how hard it was to live alone
You knew how love has hurt me
You knew your mom didn't love you.

You see that I smoke
You see that I fight
But you don't know me.

You would know me if
You knew how I turn emotions to haze
You knew how I don't fear death
You knew how tucked in the corner was sadness.
  —by a young man in juvenile detention, age thirteen

Writing personal poetry is transformative for teens at risk. The writing process helps teens who have experienced childhood traumas such as abuse and neglect begin to articulate, in a safe way, what they've been through and how they feel. At the same time, the teens feel better after writing and learn how to use writing as a tool for future healing.

The outcomes of writing for these youth include discovering an outlet for difficult emotions, developing new language skills, finding creative joy, improving communication on painful topics, and building closer relationships.

Young people who are in distress from abuse/neglect and similarly affecting trauma are the "teens at risk" under discussion here. These youth deeply want the self-exploratory and self-disclosive capabilities of expressive writing, even though they may not recognize this until they've written their first poem.

The Pongo Teen Writing Project

I founded the Pongo Teen Writing Project ("Pongo") in 1995[1] to provide poetry-writing experiences inside juvenile detention centers, homeless shelters, psychiatric hospitals, and other sites. Teams of trained volunteers ("mentors") meet weekly for six months with youth ("authors"). Our mission is to help distressed youth, through expressive writing, to better understand their feelings, build self-esteem, and take increased control of their lives. As of 2012, we have worked with six thousand teens, about half in individual sessions and the remainder in groups.

Pongo prioritizes working with youth who have a hard time expressing themselves, as we believe that the *least* articulate teens find it *most* transformative to express personal pain creatively. When we go into a classroom within the institution to seek youth for a writing session, we do not ask, "Who wants to write poetry today?" Rather, we ask, "Who hasn't written poetry before?" About one-third of the youth we serve have "never or seldom" written expressively, according to our exit surveys. Our protocol also prioritizes providing a writing experience to as many different teens as possible within our sites. Therefore, many teens experience writing with Pongo only once, yet they are very positively affected, based on our surveys, research, and reports from the teens' therapists.

The consistent theme of our teens' writing is childhood traumas. While these topics are difficult, the teens report feeling relieved, proud, even elated by their creative process. About 99 percent willingly contribute their finished work for possible inclusion in one of Pongo's published chapbooks,[2] which are distributed free to the youth that we serve, as well as to libraries, agencies, judges, therapists, and others. The books are also displayed and sold at arts festivals, where Pongo has shared our authors' poetry with ten thousand people in the Seattle and greater Washington community.

Poetry as Expressive Writing

There are three primary reasons why Pongo uses poetry as our sole expressive writing medium.

First, a teen is able to complete a poem with a mentor every time, even when the writing time is as little as thirty-five minutes. The authors always have the opportunity to experience success, contributing to personal validation and encouragement for future self-expression.

The Typical Pongo Teen Author

- He is in juvenile detention, in-patient psychiatric treatment, homeless shelter, or another institutional setting.
- She has experienced abuse and neglect.
- She is between the ages of twelve to eighteen.
- He is equally likely to have written poetry "never" or "seldom" (one-third), "some" (one-third), or "a lot" (one-third).
- She has difficulty articulating thoughts and feelings surrounding the complexity of her family situation and current life circumstances.
- He enjoys, benefits from, and is pleased with poems that he writes with Pongo mentors.

Second, poetry is an economic medium in which imagery and rhythm communicate emotional subtlety and depth. These qualities can be expressed on the page even when writing precedes a teen's conscious understanding of the experience. This subtlety is important for youth in a variety of emotional binds, such as experiencing complicated feelings of deep love for family members who may have betrayed them. When an author can turn her complex emotions into poetic images, such as comparing love to drowning in an ocean, she often learns something through poetry that she would have difficulty knowing in any other way.

Third, poetry moves naturally, intuitively, and quickly toward resolution—a final, climactic (though sometimes delicate) revelation. The revelation, representing a shift in understanding, may be a positive outcome, an expression of the deepest hurt, the observation of complexity, or the formulation of a question. The teens' poems wind out in this way.

For example, one teen told us he was confused. We asked him to list for us, one at a time, some of the things that confused him, and we used his list to construct a poem. The teen spoke about the medication he was on, his drug

Pongo Teen Authors
Survey Results

From 726 surveys of teen authors, fall 2005 to spring 2012:

- 100 percent enjoyed the writing experience
- 98 percent were proud of their writing
- 73 percent wrote on topics they don't normally talk about
- 83 percent said that writing made them feel better
- 75 percent learned about themselves
- 86 percent learned about writing
- 94 percent said they expected to write more in the future
- 92 percent said they expected to write when life is difficult

problem, and the circumstances of his arrest. We asked for one more confusing thing that we could use to end his poem. He shared his memory of the last time he saw his father, when his dad threw him "through a sheetrock wall."

When teens write from the heart about a terrible experience, the experience becomes externalized and concrete. The fog of shame and confusion lifts, and the experience is objectified as a real, though often painful, event that can be better comprehended both emotionally and cognitively. Essential to this comprehension are the emotions that the teens include in their writing. We believe that it is this ability to integrate honest feelings with a terrible experience that brings the healing power to the poem and to the poem's author.

The poem, then, is a breakthrough in self-understanding and the source of creative pride that often leads to sharing, communication, and more open relationship with supportive adults.

Dear Mom
I just thought you should know that life is hard—I've seen a lot:
murders, love like grandma's peanut butter pancakes, hate like my parents'
addiction and absence, my siblings tormenting me because I have a different
dad (theirs sent money, mine disappeared)

I'm loud, but it's a mask
On the inside I'm quiet
But I'm making sure I'm seen *and* heard

I just thought you should know that your actions make me hate you, every-
thing you made me see—it made me think you didn't care: taking me to
drug houses, letting people do what they wanted to me so you could score

I'm going to be more than you were
I'm going to make you proud of me

I just thought you should know that I love you and that the pain that you
caused taught me a lesson—about how to treat my children:
I'll never do to them what you did to me

I'm going to help them succeed
—by a young woman in juvenile detention, age sixteen

Introducing Expressive Writing

The teen authors we work with are fairly typical of institutionalized adoles-cents, and we find that youth in juvenile detention, in-patient psychiatric treatment, shelters, and other sites have an inherent impulse to understand and explain their lives. However, this impulse sometimes meets resistance. We actively work to lower that resistance in the way we initially describe the writing program to youth.

We introduce ourselves to youth with our core concept: "Write from the heart about who you are as a person." We say, "Honesty is the most important quality of good writing." We explain our belief that "people who have led dif-ficult lives have important things to say." We invite them into the experience of writing a poem about their lives, with the understanding that they will have help from a mentor. We tell them not to be concerned about things such as spelling or grammar.

Then we read some poems from one of Pongo's published chapbooks. When the youth hear heartfelt poetry by their peers, they often find that their own emotions are more accessible. They may feel a vicarious open-

---

Profile of a Mentor

- Capable of introspective process
- Knows and continues to learn about own vulnerabilities
- Can translate self-awareness into empathy
- Has clear boundaries
- Seeks peer support for difficult work

ness and creativity. They recognize that they are not alone, that universal experiences can be expressed in ways that are uniquely individualized, and that others like them write poems that explore important themes in evocative ways.

After the writing session, authors are given the chance to read their poems aloud to the group, or they may ask their mentors to read. We also tell them that by the end of the day, the mentor will type up their poem and give them several clean copies. These opportunities to read and to receive copies of their finished work are rewarding for youth and their mentors.

What It's Like to Have a Headache

When I woke up I had a headache.
It felt like Bulldozing a rock.
I wonder if I think too hard.
I wonder if playing too much tackle football
gives me these excruciating headaches.
I wonder if the headache will ever go away.
I wonder if my Dad is doing OK now,
working hard, watching my L'il sisters.
So much responsibility, Learning to take
care of his loved ones.
I wonder if he will ever change his ways,
Watching us while Drinking,
bringing other Females in while Mom is gone
or Doing Crank in the bathroom not knowing
who us kids are when he comes out.
As I get older I wonder why
he did these things???
Did he really mean what he says
about how he loves us so much???
As I wake out of my daze there it is
Another headache.
—by a young woman in juvenile detention, age sixteen

Accepting Self-Expression

The first step in helping teens write poetry is *accepting self-expression*—helping the author feel as if both he and his words are safe and respected. There are four core qualities for accepting self-expression:

- Listening to what teens have to say
- Valuing teens' creative work and effort
- Sharing teens' work with others (with permission)
- Not criticizing, but rather, encouraging

Here's an example of how the simple act of accepting self-expression can make a difference. One of the language arts teachers in juvenile detention began saving the poetry that teens brought to him, poems facilitated by Pongo mentors and by other teachers. Whenever a student in his classes finished an assignment early, the teacher would show the student a three-ring binder of other teens' poetry. He would invite the teen to write her own original poetry for the binder. With this simple support, teens began writing more and sharing their work. The teacher became a locus of poetry in the school, just by welcoming, sharing, and "publishing" student work.

Figure 8.1 illustrates accepting self-expression as part of a sequence of teaching methods.

Listening

The ability to listen is the single most important quality that a mentor brings to a writing session. We define *listening* as serious attention infused with feeling and empathy, and absent of directive efforts toward behavioral change. The mentor's ability to simply listen empathically, without judgment, allows the author to express herself freely and openly.

Valuing

Valuing is the quality of affirming the teen's poem and process with attention and appreciation *in the moment*. Valuing involves recognition of the remarkable act of taking risks and sharing in the process. It also involves appropriate praise, pointing out specific qualities of the poem—even if it is only a single

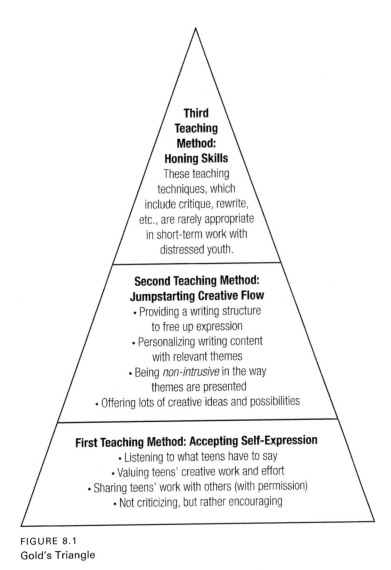

**Third
Teaching
Method:
Honing Skills**
These teaching
techniques, which
include critique, rewrite,
etc., are rarely appropriate
in short-term work with
distressed youth.

**Second Teaching Method:
Jumpstarting Creative Flow**
• Providing a writing structure
to free up expression
• Personalizing writing content
with relevant themes
• Being *non-intrusive* in the way
themes are presented
• Offering lots of creative ideas and possibilities

First Teaching Method: Accepting Self-Expression
• Listening to what teens have to say
• Valuing teens' creative work and effort
• Sharing teens' work with others (with permission)
• Not criticizing, but rather encouraging

FIGURE 8.1
Gold's Triangle

word, phrase, image, or metaphor—that are effective, unique, creative, and honest.

Valuing also involves patience and appreciation for the stages it sometimes takes to develop trust. A teen may begin his creative efforts by testing the poetry waters and offering a poem that is less personal. A young man at the state psychiatric hospital sat down with a mentor in a one-on-one session and began his dictation by reading from a dictionary. The mentor understood the need. At the next writing session, the teen wrote a poem about finding the body of a friend who had committed suicide.

Sharing

The opportunity to share what she has written validates, supports, and encourages a young writer. Earned applause and genuine affirmation are potent rewards for teens at risk. If it is realistic to type and return printed copies of an author's poem, it sends a significant message to a child who may never have had a parent proudly display artwork or schoolwork on the family refrigerator. There are many ways that a facilitator can recognize young authors: posting work on a bulletin board, publishing a poem in a newsletter, creating a poem notebook, arranging readings, providing recognition, or creating a stapled, photocopied chapbook of contributed works.

Not Criticizing

For teen writers, the most important message—a message that can make a tremendous difference to them in their future personal development and academic progress—is that *their self-expression has value.* Thus, critiquing teens' work is rarely appropriate. At-risk teens, who may well already feel a crippling amount of shame, must first believe in their voices before feeling the burden of the skills they lack. There is ample opportunity to teach skills that can make writing more successful once teens have developed some confidence and a belief in expressive writing.

That said, there are significant ways to suggest changes in a teen's writing that will also teach new skills. If an adult responds to poetry from the perspective of an inquisitive reader, an appreciator, or a poetry coach, a great deal of information about poetry can be communicated while holding an encouraging, nonjudgmental stance. For example:

- As a *reader*, explain to the teen that you're curious about how she felt in the circumstances she describes. A mentor can help a teen articulate feelings in her poem.
- As an *appreciator* of the poem, a mentor can ask for more examples of experiences in the teen's life, and also for more poems.

- As a *poetry coach*, a mentor can illustrate how a poetic device, such as a simile or a repeated line, can add subtlety and emotional weight to a poem. This is done with lots of examples, *specific to the poem*, so the teen can understand and create easily.

To Publish or Not to Publish?

Many agencies are willing to sponsor chapbooks or collections of teen writing. These can range from a stapled, photocopied collection to actual print-on-demand books.

- First and foremost consideration: Evaluate the best interests of the teen authors. Do they hope to reconcile with family members they are writing about? Is there any chance this poem in print could interfere with that hope?
- Be mindful of legal requirements that protect the confidentiality of minors.
- Honor teens' copyright rights to their own creative works. Authors own their creative work and must give permission for publication. We note on the copyright page that "copyright for the poems themselves remain in the name of the individual authors."
- Obtain written permission from all authors. Release forms can be presented at the time the poem is written with the clear disclosure that publication is a possibility and not a promise.
- Never use real names. We believe this general policy is an appropriate protection for our vulnerable authors.
- If the publication is being coordinated with an agency, close cooperation is required. Agencies may be understandably anxious about a publication project, and it is appropriate to address concerns and communicate with individuals on many levels in an organization.
- Always consider publication thoughtfully. Pongo began by consulting with community psychiatrists, agencies, and a copyright attorney, as well as seeking feedback from youth.

The significant role here for the adult is that he is *not* pointing out "mistakes" in order to make the poem better. He is pointing out things he likes, helping a young person succeed as a poet, and always expressing a wish for more writing.

Doors of Emotion
I'm opening up closed doors
Behind one door I find sadness
It's blue, it's boring, it's lonely, it makes you cry

Behind another door
You see happy people enjoying things they like
You hate them because they're happy, and you're not
So you slam the door and move to the next one

The next door is terrifying
You see guns and drugs and people dying
It's a dangerous door to walk through

There's a door in my heart
It's so full that when you open it
Everything comes tumbling down
All the frustrations, the joys, the hate, the love

Somewhere in there is the perfect life
A perfect me
—a young woman in juvenile detention, age fifteen

Jump-Starting Creative Flow

At Pongo, we believe that the desire to heal oneself through self-expression is a natural and transformative part of being human. Creativity flows naturally for teens, like water flowing downhill, except that people often need help to remove the dams of doubt, fear, and unconscious resistance. This unblocking

Pain into Poetry: The Role of the Mentor

The role of the mentor is *not* to counsel, give advice, or develop relationships beyond the role of writing facilitator. Rather, the role of the mentor is to be a deep listener, a talented teacher, and an advocate of the value of expressive writing. The role of the mentor is to help youth transform pain into poetry through empathic resonance, helping the author translate and channel the pain into a poem, and then bearing witness to the finished work.

Pongo mentors go through training to learn the program's teaching methods and facilitation techniques, as well as protocols for the mentor's emotional management and self-care. Mentors are often left with residual feelings after actively witnessing the raw pain and struggle of the teens' stories, and, because of confidentiality commitments, they are limited in how and with whom they can share. To support their emotional well-being, Pongo places all mentors on a peer team. Teams meet before and after each session to plan, exchange stories, release emotions, give and receive support, and write and share their own poems.

Mentors are trained to respond appropriately to legal and ethical "duties to report" situations in which a teen is in danger, or is a danger to himself or to others.

is made easier when the writing process is *doable, relevant, safe,* and *open.* We call that *jump-starting creative flow.*

When creative flow is jump-started, the teens learn that expressive writing is a great need and a great gift. They learn that they can succeed in expressing their deepest thoughts and feelings in a poem.

There are four aspects of jump-starting creative flow:

- Providing a writing structure to free up self-expression
- Personalizing writing content with relevant themes
- Being nonintrusive in the way we present themes and options
- Offering lots of creative ideas and possibilities

See figure 8.1, where these methods are illustrated as part of a sequence of teaching techniques.

Providing a Writing Structure

Pongo helps youth to write by providing a structure in which self-expression, even on personal and difficult themes, is natural and unencumbered. The art of this structure is that it removes the fear and doubt that might be engendered by sitting in front of a blank piece of paper. Instead, the structure makes personal written communication as easy as a conversation—with natural content, an encouraging emotional tone, a comfortable setting, an interested and supportive mentor, and no expectations.

For example, one of the structures in Pongo's program is a fill-in-the-blank poem. Teens are given sentence stems and asked to complete them with one or several responses. In the writing activity "Ten Reasons to Love Me," there are lines such as

I may not be perfect, but I can _____

I want the people around me to understand _____

I have unusual ideas, like _____

I have a secret talent. I can _____

You can see how much easier it might be for a teen to write about herself in this way, especially if she normally struggles with feeling unlovable. Here, she doesn't have to confront self-doubts about her ability or her worth. In a process like this fill-in-the-blank activity, a teen can express, recognize, and share some of her aspirations and gifts, even when she might never have expressed them before. Additionally, fill-in-the-blank activities frequently offer structures to include both the bad and the good in a situation, thus giving voice to the dualities and conflicts inherent in relationships, environments, and choices.

The same process works to facilitate sadder and more challenging feelings that are at the emotional core of teens at risk. Figure 8.2, the fill-in-the-blank example at the end of this chapter, was inspired by the teen poem that opens the chapter and is on the theme of feeling misunderstood. The structure of the exercise, including the poetic repetition and rhythm, sets an emotional tone for the teen and makes direct communication easier. Through the interactive version of this poem on its website, Pongo has received multiple versions of this completed exercise, powerful poems in which teens say, "You would know me if . . ." you knew about the secret world of abuse at home. Many of the fill-in-the-blank poems are easy to facilitate in either a group or one-on-one session.

Another structure, specific to one-on-one sessions, is *taking dictation*. With a pad and pen (or laptop) in hand, the mentor sits with a teen. The mentor asks the teen if there's anything on her mind, and when she speaks, he writes down what she says. The mentor asks clarifying questions and offers suggestions. The mentor's involvement makes the process both conversational and personal. The mentor interacts collaboratively to ask for elaboration on important points, about how the teen felt in a situation, and what happened next. The mentor's coaching on poetic device (for instance, use of line breaks, poetic imagery, repetition, and sensory details) can give the teen's words a poetic rhythm and emotional power. But mostly, the teen has a context in which to tell her story without judgment. This is the essential process.

Personalizing Writing Content

The teens with whom Pongo works have often suffered horrific traumatic experiences: watching Mom being beaten regularly by her boyfriend, seeing a cousin murdered on the streets, being raped, having an alcoholic father walk out forever, having parents who feed their addictions instead of feeding their children.

Teens at risk need the opportunity to write about *themselves*; it is important to provide writing topics that speak to the teens' personal issues. These issues are psychologically, philosophically, and spiritually profound. How does the teen really feel about the events around him? How does she explain and make sense of the experiences she's had? How does he begin to understand intensely mixed feelings? What are her wishes and regrets? What are his strengths? How does she imagine a future? How does he find meaning in his life?

Pongo has dozens of writing activities to help teens feel safe in expressing important experiences and feelings, and new titles are constantly added. These structures are available on the Pongo website and include titles such as:

- Addicted
- Where I Come From
- Lessons of Courage and Fear
- Inside Me
- When Death Comes Suddenly
- Walk One Mile in My Shoes
- This Is Who You Are to Me

Being Nonintrusive

Creating an opportunity for deep personal expression, *while purposefully being nonintrusive*, is a baseline intention for Pongo mentors. While teens need the resilience that expressive writing can help develop, they do *not* need compulsory reenactments of trauma. There is an important distinction between encouraging teens to express what they need to express and confronting them with the terror that has enshrouded them.

How does one encourage writing about abuse and neglect without intruding?

No teen in the Pongo program is ever required or pressured to write about his hurt. No teen ever hears that "it would be good for her" or that she "should" or "must" write about something painful. Instead, teens hear, "Write from the heart about who you are," or "Write about what's on your mind." He is offered models and examples of personal expression. She is always in charge of the topic and of what she discloses.

There is often an evolution to writing openly. Some teens begin by expressing something that seems superficial, such as feeling bored in detention. The mentor will always begin a poem where the teen begins her thoughts. A modest beginning will often lead to deeper topics, sometimes in the same poem. For example, a teen who writes about her boredom and frustration in detention may also bring up mixed feelings about the world outside detention, or the numbness that lurks just beyond the boredom.

Even a personalized writing activity that addresses a teen's emotional preoccupations can be offered without directly confronting his trauma or the betrayal it might contain. For example, if the teen were offered an opportunity to write about "mother," the suggestion would not be, "Write about the worst thing your mother ever did" or even "Write about your mother." Instead, he might be invited to "Write down some questions you have about mothers in general, such as 'Why do mothers . . .'"

Are There Risks to Vulnerable Youth?

Trauma specialists may ask whether Pongo authors, many of whom have only one experience with a mentor writing a poem, may have residual "emotional backlash"—reactivation of injuries and hurts that have been locked inside, or a struggle to manage, process, and resolve feelings that arose during the poem-making process. What happens to the author when the mentor leaves? Does the author feel exposed, vulnerable, alone, and without resources for coping?

Not according to the adults who work with them. Dr. Miral Luka conducted a research project on Pongo at Child Study and Treatment Center (CSTC), the Washington State psychiatric hospital for children. She noted that in addition to writing about important core issues, the youth at CSTC used their poetry to relate positively to others within the institution. Jennifer Heger, a counselor for homeless youth at Orion Center, said, "I don't recall any backlash of emotions. I think this is because the author controls the experience. Inherently, the kids can only write as deeply as they are ready for therapeutically, developmentally, cognitively. It's a readiness issue. They titrate it themselves."

Vicki Belluomini, head of mental health programs at Echo Glen Juvenile Rehabilitation Center, reported "continued growth and forward progress. The group didn't just stir up feelings and give no way to express them. The writing itself, and fully experiencing the feelings using this modality, is the soothing."

Dr. Mick Storck, a psychiatrist at CSTC, considered the two hundred Pongo authors there. "I could probably recall 30, 40, maybe 50 kids who brought their poems in for me to read—including poems that criticized me or the hospital!"

One healing power of poetry, according to Dr. Storck, may exist in the dynamic tension between separation and union. According to Dr. Storck, the Pongo authors believe that their personal writing is also a help to others, serving a greater good. "The kids who participated in poetry enjoyed camaraderie, group productivity, and social generosity," he said.

Offering Lots of Creative Ideas

The nature of creativity is actually quite different from the way some people would describe individual accomplishment. Some people expect creators to work in isolation, without the influence of others, in order to achieve great things. This theory seems to be that to work collaboratively might be a form of cheating that could lower the measure of an individual's ability.

Actually, creativity is often highly stimulated by others. Creativity is often a riff on many influences in a creator's life. The more powerfully the ideas flow in the creator's environment, the more powerfully they affect constructively the artist's creativity.

A Pongo mentor will not hesitate to provide examples of images, sensory details, and themes, especially if a writer seems to be at a loss for her own words. Typically the writer won't actually select one of the suggested ideas but will use the ideas to stimulate her own creative process. The mentor may ask, "Is your anger like a forest fire, or a volcano?" The teen may respond, "No, my anger is like a snake that turns around and bites me."

Steps for Expressive Writing with Teens at Risk

If you are interested in working with kids at risk, but you are not certain how to get started, here are some ideas.

Teachers, therapists, youth workers, and poets/writers are often naturals for this work. If you are tentative because you haven't worked with youth at risk, or because you don't have any experience with poetry, start small and build up.

If you don't have facilitation experience, get some baseline training. See the Resources section at the end of this chapter for suggestions.

You can begin by reading and sharing poetry with teens. There are many teen poems and templates at the Pongo website that can be printed out, shared, and discussed with individuals and groups. At the same time, you can invite youth to share any writing they may have already done, perhaps in journals, as song lyrics, or in academic classes. Later, you can introduce writing activities from Pongo or other sources to generate original, new poems.

If you come to a social service agency from the outside, you can begin by volunteering within the agency's school, working alongside an experienced teacher. In collaboration with the teacher, you can begin by reading and sharing poetry. Again, you can use poetry from the Pongo site, or from the adult's own inventory of poetry selected for teens at risk (see chapter 5 for guidelines for literature selection). The progression then moves to inviting teens to share their own poems. Later, the agency may align with you in starting a regular writing group.

The Pongo method supports safe practices. It is not a mentor's role to develop a personal relationship with youth. The mentor's role is to be a good listener and a good facilitator of the writing process.

Pongo has seen that people with relatively little experience can establish exciting and powerful writing programs for teens who have been terribly hurt in their lives. With these methods, you may enjoy success quickly; teens often become enthusiastic writers. They can be helped. And you may feel amply rewarded. You might be inspired to create your own unique writing activities. Perhaps soon after, you might start to think about organizing community readings, publishing chapbooks, inviting guest poets, and expanding the healing power of poetry into the lives of teens at risk.

Conclusion

The Pongo Teen Writing Project has demonstrated for many years, and across many forums, that teens at risk benefit tremendously from even one exposure to writing poems about their lives. A nonjudgmental, affirming mentor, one who encourages and accepts free expression and uses a variety of proven methods to jump-start the author's creative flow, enhances the benefit of the experience. Pongo continues to fulfill its mission to serve youth through poetry, and to serve mentors through training, support, and opportunities to make a difference in the lives of at-risk teens.

Monkey
Dedicated to my little sister

When Mom's not home we go to the park
and pick the plums from the trees
you like the small ones but I say
they're not quite ready yet, they're sour
but you say you like it, you like the sour ones

The plums aren't there anymore
all of them fell three weeks before I came here
we went back to the park
and the plums were all fallen
all rotten

It will be summer the next time
we go to get plums from the park
you'll be six and want to climb the trees
to get them—you also like
bananas, so I call you Monkey

I miss you
—a young man in juvenile detention, age twelve

Resources

Pongo Teen Writing Project website, www.pongoteenwriting.org. There are many teen poems and about fifty structured activities on the site. The poems can all be printed out. The activities can all be downloaded for use in the classroom or writing group. Also, if the teens have access to computers, the activities can be completed online, perhaps in the company of a caring adult.

When a poem is created online at the Pongo website, the youth have the options to print out their poems, email their poems, and share their poems with Pongo. Note that teen poems submitted on the Pongo site are not automatically shared publicly. After review, a few teen poems are posted, but only with permission, and only anonymously.

Pongo Teen Writing Project Mentor Training. Sign up for email notification at www.pongoteenwriting.org. Once or twice a year, training for new volunteers is offered in Seattle for a modest cost. Prospective mentors are trained in the methods of accepting self-expression and jump-starting creative flow, including the techniques of facilitating fill-in-the-blank poems, taking dictation, and other methodologies. Pongo also offers presentations and workshops at conferences and for agencies.

National Federation for Biblio/Poetry Therapy, www.NFBPT.com. The nonprofit credentials board for the field offers in-depth training in the facilitation of poetry therapy. Distance or in-person training is completed with an approved mentor/supervisor who oversees a guided independent study program.

Therapeutic Writing Institute, www.TWInstitute.net. Completely online professional training program with courses in therapeutic writing theory and practice, professional development, and psychological awareness. Several poetry classes are offered. Quarterly eight-week terms. Reasonable tuition. Continuing education certificates available for counselors. TWI has received endorsement by the National Federation for Biblio/Poetry Therapy as a standards-based credentials-granting institute.

Name:

Date:

YOU DON'T KNOW ME

Activity Instructions: The purpose of this activity is to explain who you are, beyond what people might see on the surface. Read the poem below, and then, on the next page, fill in the blanks to create a poem of your own.

HOW TUCKED IN THE CORNER
by Chuck

You see that I'm alone
You see that I steal
But you don't know me.

You would know me if
You knew how hard it was to live alone
You knew how love has hurt me
You knew your mom didn't love you.

You see that I smoke
You see that I fight
But you don't know me.

You would know me if
You knew how I turn emotions to haze
You knew how I don't fear death
You knew how tucked in the corner was sadness.

FIGURE 8.2
Sample Pongo Teen Writing Activity

Fill in the blanks below to create your own poem. Use the words suggested or choose your own words to communicate your thoughts as clearly and powerfully as you can. Feel free to add lines, remove lines, or make any other changes that fit your purpose.

YOU DON'T KNOW ME

You see that I _____
                                (fight, ???)
You see that I _____
                                (do what people want, ???)
But you don't know me

You would know me if ...

You knew how hard it was to _____
                                (hold in my anger, ???)
You knew how I feel sometimes that _____
                                (no one cares, ???)
You knew how _____
                                (my dad walked out on me, ???)

You see that I _____
                                (swear, ???)
You see that I _____
                                (smoke, ???)
But you don't know me

You would know me if ...

You knew how I _____
                                (express myself through art, ???)
You knew how I _____
                                (like to cook, ???)
You knew how I _____
                                (take care of my younger sisters, ???)

Notes

1. The use of collective pronouns *we, our,* and *us* refers to the Pongo team: mentors, other volunteers, and me, the creative and executive director.

2. Most of Pongo's chapbooks are about sixty-four pages. They are professionally printed and saddle stitched (bound along the centerline) with wire staples. More recent books are perfect bound (typical paperbacks with a glued spine).

9

Writing Your Family Story

LINDA JOY MYERS

I'm lying in a feather bed in an upstairs bedroom with my great-grandmother, Blanche. Lights from the highway sweep across the angled ceiling above the bed as she begins to whisper the stories of her life, her teeth in a jar by the bed. I'm eight and she's eighty and it's the first time I've met her. She's my grandmother's mother—I live with Gram, since my parents have not been able to take care of me. My mother left when I was four, and for the first time today, I find out there is a huge family I'm related to—Gram's brothers and sisters in Iowa, warm, friendly folk who smile and pat me on the back, surrounding me with a web of family that is so new I can hardly believe it.

Blanche begins to tell me the stories of her life in the mid-19th century—she was born three years before Custer's Last Stand. She was the first of six children, young and barefoot, picking up the back-breaking work of farm women—raising gardens and children, canning and baking, serving the farm hands, washing clothes in a pot in the yard. Blanche's hands are working hands, and she folds them over her chest as she talks.

"I delivered the babies too, and I'll never fergit"—she says it like that—"the first time I heard a voice over a telephone. I cried. And the radio—the first time . . ." her voice dims while she stirs her memories. I prod her to go on, trying to understand who she is, and where we came from. "You're Gram's mama? Did you know my Mama?"

"Lands sake, girl. I'm Lulu's Mama, all right. I knew your Mama—Jo'tine we called her—when she was a little girl, sweet thing she was." I think about my beautiful mother I miss so much, her dark eyes and pretty face, but sometimes

she doesn't seem to see me. "Lulu's Papa, Louis was his name—we got married
on a snowy New Year's Day, 1894, and two months later he died of pneumonia."

I could see it—the snowy day, the squeak of saddle leather on the horses,
the crunch of hooves, Blanche's face smooth and young, as I try to imagine the
woman I know as my grandmother being a little baby.

"It was all so long ago. We worked hard, we women was midwives to each
other, and there was all the cannin' and the bakin.' Sweatin' at the cook stove.
Things was different then. Land sakes."

In the silence I understand as I look at her ancient body that Blanche is a walk-
ing storybook. She knows eight decades of history. She's the mother of the mother
of the mother, and knows everything. I have to find out what she knows—why did
my mother leave me and why did my grandmother leave my mother? I want to
understand the birthing of babies and canning in the summer and how you light
a fire in the wood cook stove.

Something magical happens when a family story is written down. Long-
buried truths pop through layers of memory. Insights unlock the authentic
self. Old stories glow through softened vision, or bristle with startling clarity.
When daughters, sons, fathers, mothers reach past the "given" story of their
lives to answer the core questions (*who am I? where did I come from? who are*
my people? why do we do what we do?), an alchemical blend of beings, histories, and shared experiences—a *family story*—emerges.

Writing a family story relies on the principle that within each of us is a ker-
nel of possibility and potential—we'll call it the *authentic self*—that can be cul-
tivated at any age, ideally beginning in earliest childhood. As children, though,
most of us were taught to suppress this authentic self and instead to participate
in *family myths*—the idealized, minimized, or exaggerated beliefs and expectations about *who we are and what we think, say, and do in this family.*

A family is a complex system with instinctual survival patterns that help
members deal with everyday stress as well as cope with heartbreaking losses
and devastating challenges. These patterns, as necessary as they may be in
the moment, often get habituated. The authentic self gets buried. Writing the
family story, living it, and dreaming it over a period of time can uncover years
of denial. Secrets can be transformed into new ways of feeling and thinking:
hatred can turn to love, resentment to forgiveness. Writing family stories can
reveal untapped personal power and knowledge, creating an environment for
deep healing.

My work of family storying—both as a family therapist and as a memoir-writing teacher/coach—is a part of my authentic self that never got buried. I've been collecting memories since I was a little girl galvanized by story. I learned when I was eight years old, on that feather bed with my great-grand-mother Blanche, that there are secret stories hiding in everyone, and when we learn what they are, we're released from the negative power of the past to the fresh possibilities of the present and future.

Blanche seared into me a curiosity about the past. I saw that if we could find out everything that happened to someone, we could understand him or her. Knowledge of the past held some kind of magic. In the past were answers that could explain and even change the present.

Over the next forty years, I pursued my family story in libraries and dusty courthouses and newspaper stacks. I found my own history, and in so doing the larger context for my life experience. I wrote that family story. Page by page I reconstructed the living, breathing story of the mother who birthed me, the grandmother who raised me, the mother I became, and all the complexities before, after, and in between.

Our history is alive in each of us. It is a part of us—our blood, our cells, and the silent, secret history that has shaped our family and each person in it. When we unlock these stories, we release knowledge and wisdom. We unwrap the gifts of discovery and change.

Family Patterns: Roles, Rules, and Myths

A core concept of any family story is *homeostasis*, or the maintenance of interdependence and the rules and roles that maintain that balance. Homeostasis describes how, as a system, a family must maintain a fragile balance. This balance is maintained through developing family myths, enacting static roles, and operating under mostly unconscious sets of rules. Knowing about the dynamics of homeostasis offers the opportunity to recognize, interpret, understand, or challenge family patterns.

Most people can readily identify the roles that each person in a family plays: *Dad ruled the roost. My younger brother was a clown; he was always cutting up. My sister disappeared into her books. My mother was always tired and short-tempered.* Homeostasis suggests that those roles helped each family member maintain his or her place in the ecosystem of the family.

Along with roles, each family has rules, again unconsciously designed to maintain the fragile balance. Most families have some rules that are specific (*In this family, we don't say/think/feel/do/wear that*) and some that are universal (*Don't ever tell our secrets*).

The family rules help maintain the *family myths*—the stories the family tells about itself: *We are pious. We are poor but honest. In our family, we work hard and don't complain.*

Children are shaped to perceive the world in a particular way and to absorb the patterns that protect the family members from near-constant stress. These defenses are picked up through behavioral patterning and emotional attunement, and children adapt to them in order to help maintain the homeostatic balance of the family. In other words, we are each conditioned *not* to see certain things about ourselves and our families. When we are ready to lift the veil, writing illuminates the unknown, clarifies confusion, heals unfinished business, and welcomes understanding.

The Healing Power of Writing Family Story

Research demonstrates that writing in a particular pattern about real-life difficulties or stresses, particularly those that have been suppressed or hidden, can improve health and well-being, both physical and emotional. Studies also show that writing about "the best experience of my life" or life goals are just as likely to be healing as the darker stories.[1] Therefore, look to both shadow and light to draw upon all aspects of life story as a way to connect dots, look at patterns, and write yourself into clarity, resolution, and integration. As one writer whose childhood included physical and emotional abuse describes it:

When I joined a memoir writing group and began to write my family story, nothing made sense. But I just wrote little stories, snippets, scenes. As I captured the small memories, I saw how I survived, moment to moment. I started to notice consistencies in what seemed chaotic. There was so much to learn about myself: who I was then, who I am now, who I become when I slow down and write my stories. The writing group received each story with tender words: "Oh, that sounds so hard," or "I'm so sorry that you had to experience such things." Those were words a parent would say to a small child, but I'd never heard them before. Through writing, I was seen, heard, and supported for the first time.

This story is just one of the hundreds of testimonies I've received in more than a decade of teaching memoir writing. Nearly everyone who seeks to explore their family story and their personal truths through writing discovers that stories are waiting to be born and often burst forward once given permission. Still, it can be daunting to explore the past, the family memories, and one's own guilt or responsibility. The critical voice of the internalized family, which wants to create silence and maintain the homeostasis, pops up with all the reasons not to write. But when this critical voice can be worked through and even incorporated into the text, breakthroughs occur and new insights appear about the family and the writer's role in it.

Many people who write their family story have not written anything personal before, yet they describe a "need" to write. They have a sense that something needs to be released and openly expressed. A door is opened. Out come threads of stories never before told, stories that the writer didn't know she was going to tell. These threads of stories begin to unravel layers of the family rules, roles, and myths, but without the confounding abstraction. Situations appear on the page in story form with living, breathing action, reaction, and dialogue for each family member's point of view.

When a writer, as creator of story, writes about others, he stands in their shoes and has new opportunities to see both the situation and the story more dimensionally, with greater compassion and understanding, even if agreement continues to be lacking. The light begins to dawn about who they were, the circumstances of their lives, why they might be the way they were, and the trajectory of their own life path.

Writing a story means that balanced weight must be given to character development, point of view, dialogue, and progression of the story for everyone in it. This discipline changes the writer. Transformation happens through this process even if the person had no intention of changing their mind about anything. If we get on the path and begin telling our story, new landscapes appear before us with opportunities to resolve our family's past and our role in it.

Witnessing and Healing in Story Writing

Another aspect of the healing power of writing lies in enlightened or compassionate witnessing and being witnessed. A counselor or teacher can be an enlightened witness—one who sees and knows the truth about the child or person, someone who holds a place for that person's authentic self. As we write our stories, we become witness to ourselves. We see and know the depth of the story being told, and we hold a space for new insights, compassion, and understanding for the protagonist, who is also the writer.

This dual consciousness helps to create a space where a new story and a new sense of self can develop. Writers of a family story begin to see the family's past objectively as they witness themselves, and they may come to see the family with perspective and even compassion over time. This is freeing, and it offers the opportunity to cut the old psychic bonds and create new pathways in the mind and in the heart that can help not only the current generation but also generations into the future. The writer creates a new legacy through writing, witnessing, and authoring a new story.

Writing Your Family Story

To write your family story, you must give yourself permission to experiment and to try new things. The techniques that follow are tried-and-true ways to begin and deepen into story, even if you're new to this kind of writing. Experiment. When you get a scene or a moment in mind, just "free write" it—write as fast as you can, even if it doesn't make sense. With your notebook, journal, or screen as companion, let's start with some of the ways you can begin writing your family story.

The Power of a Scene

In this chapter's opening scene, two people—an old woman and a young girl—are sharing family stories. The scene quickly sets us in a place (*I'm lying in a feather bed in an upstairs bedroom with my great-grandmother, Blanche*) and a time (*I'm eight and she's eighty*). As the scene continues, we experience the old woman's folk wisdom and the child's explosion of curiosity. Details—dialects, dates, activities—bring the scene alive.

Writing in scene is the most powerful way to bring yourself fully into the lived world of story. It evokes a simultaneous reality of you, the present self, telling the story of the lived moment of your past self's experience.

In a scene, sensual details such as sight, sound, smell, and a kinesthetic sense bring the scene alive. Colors, texture, and aromas lead to reexperienced emotions.

Eight Truths about Scenes

1. A scene takes place at a certain time and place. It is presented in "real time."
2. A scene *shows* (Blanche's teeth in a jar) more than it *tells* (Blanche is eighty).
3. A scene has a specific story to tell about something that must be experienced fully.
4. A scene includes characters who want something, who are passionate about what they want, and who often have a conflict.
5. A scene includes sensual details—the visceral feel, smell, taste, sight, sound.
6. A scene may include dialogue.
7. The events that happen in a scene move along the plot of the story.
8. A scene is a bead on the string of the narrative line.

As writer, you are the "I" character in the story and at the same time the one who reflects on what is being presented. *I went to my grandmother's house that day, and picked strawberries, but I wondered what kind of mood she'd be in. I always had to keep an eye out for her moods.*

This dual consciousness offers a way to witness the story as an adult while reentering the world of the past. Seemingly magical insights can arise with this juxtaposed reality of now and then, present and past.

Writing in scene begins by simply remembering. Bring to mind a family story. Let it play out visually; see the movie of this memory in your imagination. When you're ready to write, begin your scene by describing the physical or emotional environment. Then narrate the story through your own experience. Writing in the present tense brings more immediacy.

Turning Points

A simple way to drop into story is to list ten to twenty of the most significant moments in your life, the *turning points* that made the difference in the trajectory of your life. This process helps focus attention on memories that matter and creates a comfortable number of starting places. Ideally there will be reasonable balance between brighter and darker memories so that the full range of experience is represented.

Then choose a memory—any one will do—and write the story. Put pen to paper or fingers to keyboard and write steadily for twenty minutes. Start anywhere and follow the words, without regard for spelling, punctuation, sentence structure, or other mechanics. Notice your emotional resonance as you write: a great sense of accomplishment often arises when a person writes a story and experiences the power, voice, and freedom in writing truth.

Create a Time Line

Tape together several sheets of paper, or find a piece of poster board. Draw a horizontal line across the long side to represent chronological time. Bold, vertical lines mark five-to-ten-year periods. Use a pencil so you can erase. To put the turning-point stories on the time line, draw vertical lines with a circle at the bottom. The circles will contain the title or theme of the turning-point story. Chart all the turning-point stories on the list. Keep track of new stories on the time line as they are recalled. Forgotten memories and information will often erupt from the hidden past when relationships among events are drawn out.

The Generational Family Time Line Project

Create a time line of the entire family, going back as many generations as there are anecdotal stories. Mark birth, marriage, divorce, or/and death dates for each member of the family. Add in historical contexts. Seeing how history lines up with personal events can be powerful and illuminating. If you know some of the turning points of family members' lives, add them in. Times of mutual stress and conflict can be revealed, as well as times of happiness and contentment that may have been forgotten. Notice how many stories or significant events cluster within a single decade. This can indicate times of immense stress and growth.

Research

If your time line shows that Aunt Madge lost a leg to polio in the 1916 epidemic, or that your great-grandfather was a fur trader on the Canadian border, harvest some details and context to weave into your story. Do Internet research, or, if you prefer the quaint twentieth-century practices, go to the library. You can quickly educate yourself on the history of an epidemic, industry, region, town, national climate, weather pattern, political context, or natural disaster. Understanding the larger context of family circumstances can bring a story to life with vibrant details. Such research can also bridge gaps, create compassion, and increase understanding of how external events and environments shaped personal and generational history.

Questions

Questions are surefire ways to reveal the family stories. You can ask these questions of yourself, or you can interview your family members to get a richer, fuller context. The questions in this section will jump-start your story process. As you ask questions of family members, be sure to respect the privacy of stories they don't want to share, and bypass questions you know will be painful or sensitive until you have built rapport and trust and can see that they are open to exploring the darker or more difficult questions.

Questions to Generate Family Stories

- What was the most courageous thing you ever did? How old were you? What was your motivation? How about the stupidest thing you ever did?
- What's the best memory of your whole life? What's the worst?
- What were your favorite stories, songs, cars, ball teams, heroes, and heroines when you were growing up? What did you love about them?
- Is there a significant date in history that has special meaning to you? Why does it have importance?
- What was the most important date in the lives of your mother and father? How about your grandmothers and grandfathers?
- What was the happiest day of your life—and why? And for your parents and grandparents?
- Think about the character traits of your mother and father—describe what makes them unique. How did they get that way? What were your parents/grandparents like as children? As teens? As young adults?
- What kind of work or career have your family members had? Was work a vocation, a career, or a paycheck? What are the employment/unemployment stories in your family?
- What was the best year of your life? Why? How about your parents? Grandparents?
- What are your family's food traditions? How did the traditions get created? How long have they been in place?
- What is the family's position on religion and spiritual practice? Is regular worship or study a part of the family norm? Has religious/spiritual practice been left behind? Has participation in religious practice and its communities been an important story thread?
- What illnesses or hospitalizations have happened in the family? Who was involved and what happened?
- What are the births, marriages, divorces, deaths, and other transitions in this family? What happened as a result of a particular transition?

- What activities have united this family in the past? How about in the present?
- What are the current, and past, stressors or worries in this family?
- What is the best thing happening to the family now?
- What hopes, plans, and positive futures is the family creating?
- How does each family member express creatively?
- What are the stories of strength in the family? What strengths does each family member bring?
- How does the family define and show love?

Every Picture Tells a Story

The right picture may indeed be worth one thousand words of family story. Here's how to use artwork and photographs as catalysts.

If you enjoy making art, try representing a memory or family story in color and shape. A drawing, a collage, a painting, or a sculpture can reveal a great deal about perception and point of view.

Photographs can jump-start memories. Find evocative photographs from photo albums, picture boxes, and digital albums. Choose a photo to work with, and write down your first impressions—a few descriptive words about the people, setting, and occasion. If you don't know or can't remember, guess.

Next, look deeply into the photograph, noticing shadows and light, facial expressions, body language, details. What is the story this picture is telling? Write it.

Writing Your Hero Story

When Harry Potter and his friends and enemies were birthed into the culture, we watched modern mythology being written in real time. Harry is the quintessential wounded hero. He's an orphan and lives as an outcast in his remaining family. He's different. He's marked. He's the innocent target of a powerful negative energy. He faces his fears and loneliness; he learns to trust himself and others; he studies hard. He goes from a naïve, scared boy to a powerful and brave hero.

What is the "hero story" in your life? When have you been the most brave or noble? What has it required of you? How about your family members?

What are each of their hero stories? How have each of you transformed through your hero's journey?

What fictional characters (toys, animals, dolls, cartoons, storybook characters) shaped your childhood? What qualities did you admire or identify with in the characters?

Make up your own hero story. Write your own personal myth with you as the protagonist, the hero/heroine of the story. Start with "Once upon a time, there was a . . ."

Additional Creative Outlets for Stories

- Graphic novels are like literary comic books. They are wildly popular with children and teens. Helping kids write and illustrate their own graphic novels is a powerful way to engage children in family storytelling.
- Film family members telling stories, and make a movie.
- Video journaling, online journaling, blogging—new technologies make new forms of storytelling accessible for all ages.
- Decorate your refrigerator with a magnetic poetry kit.
- Cut out words and images from magazines and collage the family story.

The New Stories: Family Gratitude Stories

The "positive psychology" movement offers new ways for families and children to connect about the feelings, stories, and shared memories that build strength and a positive future for the family. In order to transition from the darker stories into more positive patterns and belief systems, new imagery and possibilities must be planted and nurtured. The ideas of forgiveness, positive functioning and roles in the family, appreciating the positive qualities of family members, and being aware of the gifts and blessings in life, no matter how small, can help to create a new way to think and feel.

Whether writing stories together or privately, the story will reflect the voice of the writer and will echo the soul of the family. A family story is like a kaleidoscope; different aspects will be visible and knowable depending on the angle of vision. It is the complex, in-the-round nature of family that makes family both so irresistible and appealing, and also so maddening and frustrating. The idea that we can have an overall view of the family composed of all the points of view without blame or criticism is to create a harmonious, live-and-let-live way to keep the family's balance in a healthy way. Perhaps story can be a way in the future that all members can have a voice and learn to respect differences.

Journals as Incubators of Story

In my family we had the rules shared by families with hidden truths and secret shames: *Children should be seen and not heard. Children have no right to privacy. Do not tell anyone what you saw/heard/felt.* So when I received a locking diary for my twelfth birthday, I knew my grandmother would read anything I wrote. I devised elaborate codes to describe my activities and companions, yet I was constricted in true expression. I yearned for the day when I could bust loose on the page, but when it was finally safe to do so, my journal entries were listless, inhibited, and fearful.

So it was an amazing revelation in the 1970s to discover the many published volumes of Anaïs Nin's diaries with her compelling woman's voice unapologetically exploring her inner and outer life. A natural storyteller, Anaïs Nin was a novelist and short story writer, and a contemporary (and, famously, a lover) of Henry Miller. Her real passion, though, was her diaries, crammed with details of her life, her wild emotions, her artist and writer friends, her work, Paris, her sexuality, world war—all in living color.

Across seven volumes spanning the years from 1931 to 1974, doors opened into her inner world as Nin painted pictures of the "real" world of wartime Europe, her competitive career, the rise of feminism, and so much more. Like many other women, reading her diaries gave me permission to write wildly, to take risks, and to explore the untouchable truths lurking dangerously and enticingly beneath the surface of my mind.

Most of us don't write journals the way Anaïs Nin did, with brilliant description and vivid color. Yet we can't overlook the power of storytelling and the ready availability of a journal to contain and preserve it. Journals—casual, immediate, portable—are the perfect media to capture fleeting bits of memories and to create on the page a whole world of smells, colors, noises, sensations, feelings. A journal is the portal to another time and place, inviting us inward and downward, revealing layers previously unspoken and unexamined as the current self meets the past self.

A journal becomes a living document in each moment of raw perception. It can be an experiment in reflection, voice, and layering down into spontaneous pops of insight. Journaling can lift the veils between the conscious and unconscious minds. We are free to play, cry, meander, and get lost in the labyrinth of reflection and remembering.

Many if not most memoirs are developed from journals, where the freedom to play and tune into the inner voice invites new layers of Self and truth to emerge. So find your voice in your journal. Take risks. Write raw. Let go. Follow Ariadne's thread into and out of the labyrinth of your family story— and perhaps into your very soul.

Note

1. See Laura A. King and Kathi N. Miner, Writing about the perceived benefits of traumatic events: Implications for physical health, *Personality and Social Psychology Bulletin* 26 (2) (2000): 220–30; Laura A. King, The health benefits of writing about life goals, *Personality and Social Psychology Bulletin* 27 (7) (2001): 798–807; and Chad M. Burton and Laura A. King, The health benefits of writing about intensely positive experiences, *Journal of Research in Personality* 38 (2) (2004): 150–63.

About the Authors

Kathleen (Kay) Adams, MA, LPC, PTR-MM/S (Preface, chapter 1, chapter 3), is a licensed professional counselor in Denver, Colorado. Since 1988 she has worked as a journal therapist in psychiatric hospitals, outpatient programs, and in private practice. She is a registered poetry/journal therapist and a master mentor/supervisor, supervising the fieldwork and study of journal/poetry therapy candidates and supervisors-in-training. She is the founder/director of the Center for Journal Therapy (www.journaltherapy.com), offering the healing art and science of journal writing to all who desire self-directed change, and in 2008 she launched its professional training division, the fully online Therapeutic Writing Institute (www.TWInstitute.net). Kay is the author of the best-selling *Journal to the Self* (1990), *The Way of the Journal* (1992, 1998), *The Write Way to Wellness* (2000), *Scribing the Soul* (2004), and five other books on therapeutic writing. She is the series editor of Rowman & Littlefield's expressive writing series and the creator of the series' website, www.Itseasytowrite.com.

Linda Barnes, MS (chapter 6), has degrees in English and psychology and is a certified poetry/journal therapist and a certified instructor of the Journal to the Self workshop. She has worked for the last twenty-four years in higher education. She has taught numerous classes and workshops on expressive writing since 1980 in Colorado, Oregon, and Arizona. Linda's personal diary extends to over thirty thousand pages. She was a contributor to Tristine Rainer's classic book, *The New Diary*, and she sponsored an appearance in Denver, Colorado, by the author Anaïs Nin, with whom she corresponded for several years. She has self-published two chapbooks of her poetry and has won several poetry awards. The Oregon Poetic Voices Project (oregonpoet-icvoices.org) recorded two of her poems, and she founded the Rogue Valley Chapter of the Oregon Poetry Association. She has coordinated the annual Southern Oregon Poetry Contest for eight years. Recently retired from her position as a community college counselor at Rogue Community College, she continues to teach a Human Potential class there each year. Linda also serves as president of the National Federation for Biblio/Poetry Therapy.

Richard Gold, MA (chapter 8), of Seattle founded the Pongo Teen Writing Project, a nonprofit group that offers unique therapeutic poetry programs to adolescents who are homeless, in jail, or in other ways leading difficult lives. In its seventeen years, Pongo has worked with over six thousand teens. The Pongo website contains writing activities for distressed youth and resources for teachers at www.pongoteenwriting.org. Prior to founding Pongo, Richard was managing editor of Microsoft Press. In 2010, Richard was named a Microsoft Integral Fellow, honored for his work with Pongo, by Bill and Melinda Gates and the Microsoft Alumni Foundation. A book of Richard's illustrated poetry, *The Odd Puppet Odyssey*, was published in 2003. In this book, the character Pongo is a puppet who struggles awkwardly with becoming human until he aspires to compassion.

Robb Jackson, MFA, PhD, CAPF, CJT (chapter 2), died in February, 2013, as this book was in production, from complications from open-heart surgery. At the time of his death, he was regents professor and professor of English at Texas A&M University-Corpus Christi. Robb's poetry originated from his journal-writing practice and was informed by close observation of his adopted home, Corpus Christi, Texas. Robb worked extensively with addicts and alcoholics in a court-ordered residential rehabilitation program where he taught poetry and journaling techniques as part of recovery. He was both a Certified Applied Poetry Facilitator (CAPF) and a Certified Journal Facilitator (CJF) and was one of the founding faculty of the Therapeutic Writing Institute. His first book of poetry, *Living on the Hurricane Coast* (2003), contains poems that stem from his transition from his northern roots to a new life along the Gulf Coast of south Texas. *Child Support* (2010) was written over a twenty-year period during and after his separation and divorce from his four children's mother. *Crane Creek, Two Voices* (2011, Fithian Press) is a collection of facing poems by Robb and his wife, Vanessa Furse Jackson. Robb served as chair of the editorial review board for this series, and his wisdom, discernment and voice will be profoundly missed.

Perie Longo, PhD, LMFT, PTR (chapter 7), is a registered poetry therapist and poet laureate *emerita* of Santa Barbara, California (2007–2009). She has taught poetry to children (K–12) through the California Poets in the Schools since 1986. In 2012, she received the Woman of Achievement Award from the Association of Women in Communication, Santa Barbara Chapter. A past president of the National Association for Poetry Therapy (2005–2007), she received their Outstanding Achievement Award (1998) and Distinguished Service Award (2004). She also is a master/mentor supervisor for those seeking credentialing through the National Federation of Biblio/Poetry Therapy. Dr. Longo has published articles on the effectiveness of poetry therapy in *The Journal of Poetry Therapy* and elsewhere. Her chapter, "Tearing the Darkness Down: Poetry as Therapy," appears in *Introduction to Alternative and Complementary Therapies*. Author of three books of poetry, the most recent of which is *With Nothing behind but Sky: A journey through grief*, her poetry appears in numerous journals and anthologies. She can be reached through her website, www.perielongo.com.

Linda Joy Myers, PhD, LCSW (chapter 9), is president of the National Association of Memoir Writers and copresident of the Women's National Book Association, San Francisco. She is the author of *The Power of Memoir: How to Write Your Healing Story*, the prize-winning memoir *Don't Call Me Mother*, and a workbook *The Journey of Memoir: The Three Stages of Memoir Writing*. She coteaches the program Write Your Memoir in Six Months with Brooke Warner. She coaches writers and offers teleseminars and workshops nationally. Linda has won prizes for fiction, memoir, and poetry. She gives workshops nationally through NAMW, Story Circle Network, and the Therapeutic Writing Institute. She can be reached through her website, www.namw.org.

Joy Roulier Sawyer, MA, LPC, PTR-M/S (chapter 5), is a registered poetry therapist and approved mentor/supervisor in private practice in Denver. Since 2003 she has cotaught masters' level writing and healing coursework with Kathleen Adams at the University of Denver. Joy has served on the boards of the National Federation for Biblio/Poetry Therapy (NFBPT) and the National Association for Poetry Therapy Foundation (NAPTF). She is currently on the editorial board for the *Journal of Poetry Therapy* and serves as Educational/Institutional Outreach chair for NAPT's board. Joy revised and updated the third edition of the academic textbook, *Biblio/Poetry Therapy—The Interactive Process: A Handbook* by Arleen McCarty Hynes and Mary Hynes-Berry (2012), for which she received the NAPT's 2013 Distinguished Service Award.

Kate Thompson, MA, CJT (chapter 4), is a senior registered BACP (British Association of Counselling and Psychotherapy) counselor and supervisor, a registered psychotherapist in the state of Colorado, and a certified journal therapist. She pioneered the use of therapeutic writing in individual counseling and for self-supervision in the UK. She is the coeditor of *Writing Works* (2006) and *Writing Routes* (2010) and the author of *Therapeutic Journal Writing: An Introduction for Professionals* (2010), all published by Jessica Kingsley Publishers, London. In 2010 Kate relocated to Boulder, Colorado, and she is now exploring the intersection of therapeutic writing and existential psychotherapy. She is core faculty for the Therapeutic Writing Institute.

Acknowledgments

Deep gratitude and appreciation to the chapter authors who have contributed such important work to the field of expressive writing and to this book. We are all blessed by your voices.

To my colleague James W. Pennebaker, abundant thanks for honoring us with a beautiful foreword.

Nancy Evans, my editor at Rowman & Littlefield, is a multiple metaphor: a rock, a beacon, an anchor. Thanks for your unflagging support, unfailing wisdom, and unerring eye.

My family supports me unconditionally. I want to particularly acknowledge my parents, Dale (d. 1992) and Theda Adams, who recognized my gifts and encouraged my talents from the very start, and who are lifelong role models of integrity, service, and generosity of heart and spirit.

Thanks to my clients, who willingly turn to the page, and who teach me how to be in better service as a journal therapist.

Thanks to my worldwide community of colleagues, friends, and students through the Center for Journal Therapy, the Therapeutic Writing Institute, the National Association for Poetry Therapy, and the National Federation for Biblio/Poetry Therapy, who continually inspire me to do my best work.

Posthumous thanks to "the Shoobeedoo Man," Robb Jackson for enriching my life and work.

I am grateful to God for a lifetime of grace, including giving me wonderful work to do, and wonderful people with whom to do it.

Kathleen Adams
June 2013